EARN YOUR STRIPES

Gold medal insights
for business and life

Neil Fachie OBE
Foreword by Sir Chris Hoy

R**Ǝ**THINK PRESS

First published in Great Britain in 2020 by Rethink Press
(www.rethinkpress.com)

Cover image © Helen Mubanga from Helen Mary Images
www.helenmaryimages.co.uk

Contents

Foreword

I've known Neil for well over a decade, the first time I met this quietly spoken Aberdonian was shortly after the 2008 Paralympics while he was still competing as a sprinter in athletics. While chatting, he dropped into the conversation that he was hoping to come down to Manchester at some point to have a go on a tandem, but in his typically understated and modest way, he made it sound like he just fancied a shot on the velodrome purely for fun.

Little did I know the next time I would see him he'd be in full kit and scorching round the boards on the back of the bike, looking like he'd done it his whole life! He was very soon part of the GB Paralympic squad and made a huge impact at his debut World Championships a few months later, winning two gold medals with his pilot Barney Storey.

With the GB Olympic and Paralympic squads training together daily in Manchester, Neil and I became team-mates, and were so until I retired in 2013. I've followed his career closely since then and watched with pride as he and Pete Mitchell became the first tandem pair ever to dip below the magical one-minute barrier for the 1000 metre time trial in 2014.

I think what has impressed me most about Neil is his steely determination and the no-nonsense way in which he takes on challenges. His visual impairment clearly hasn't stood in the way of him setting ambitious goals in life, and the methodical way in which he approaches them is clearly a big part of what has made him so successful.

Earn Your Stripes is a very honest and open account of what it took for him to become a record-breaking Paralympic and World Champion. It reveals the secrets behind his success – or rather the fact that there are no secrets – the importance of meticulous planning and good old-fashioned hard work. He realised that what he has learned, and continues to learn, from his sporting career can be applied to life beyond the velodrome by anyone, and so this book was born.

This is an incredibly helpful guide, setting out a five-step plan to be your best and achieve your goals, all told in an autobiographical way that brings each point to life in a thoroughly engaging manner. This book illustrates how his hard work, resilience and ability to re-evaluate after each Paralympic cycle have kept him at the top of his sport for over eleven years and, most importantly for you as the reader, how you can benefit from this knowledge and experience.

I have no doubt this book will be well received by all who read it, as it will inspire them to be bold, aim high, and equip them with the tools to deal with the ups and downs that life throws in the way on a daily basis. Whether it be for sport, business, or just life in general, there are practical nuggets of wisdom that shouldn't be missed.

Sir Chris Hoy
Six-times Olympic champion

Introduction

For over a decade, winning at major championships has been my career. Twenty-six medals and counting; nineteen of which are gold. Records have tumbled, opponents have been dispatched, and more often than not I've been at the top of the podium. To the onlooker it may look a little too easy, perhaps even tedious. I've been asked many times, 'What is your secret to success?' My response is that there is no secret, it's just a case of unrelenting hard work in the pursuit of my goals. In recent years, however, I've come to realise that I have, in fact, learnt a great deal about how to strategise, plan and ultimately execute under extreme pressure. Perhaps I do know a secret or two.

This book outlines the step-by-step approach I have developed over my sporting career. Even in my mid-thirties I'm still breaking records. This method doesn't just work on the velodrome, it works in the boardroom, in start-ups, in sport, wherever you choose to apply it – just ask my clients.

Don't worry, this isn't a typical in-your-face, motivational sportsperson story, I'm not that guy. I am not a positive person – I am from Scotland! I worry what people think about me, stress about missing a train and usually consider all the problems I might encounter before deciding whether to meet with friends. What you don't get from this book is a peppy, 'Think it and you can be it' approach. I am a realist and as such I don't believe in quick fixes, hacks or shortcuts. I may not be your typical personal development author, but perhaps that makes me the ideal person to help guide you towards a more successful path in your chosen field.

By overcoming serious self-confidence issues to compete on a global stage, adapting my life to cope with a degenerative eye condition, and learning from my various failures, I have become the best in the world at what I do. I chose to write this book because I want to share what I've learnt with people like me. Shy, ordinary people who work hard but lack the confidence to step out from the crowd and show the world what they're capable of.

During my sporting career I've had many highs and lows. In the early days there were plenty more lows than highs. The beauty of these struggles is that each one taught me something about myself and helped me in my battle to reach the top. I am under no illusions, I'm pretty ordinary. I am self-critical and suffer from self-doubt; new things scare me. Despite this, I have learnt how to get the most out of myself, how to use my weaknesses to my advantage. As well as sharing my stories, this book outlines the processes I have learnt along the way.

The processes have nothing to do with physical effort or training techniques, instead I look at the mental aspect. How I find the motivation to push myself. What thought processes are required to overcome barriers. What steps I must take to move forward. This book answers all these questions and more using what I have learnt from the world of elite sport.

There is a common misconception that to be successful in sport – or life in general – you need to be mentally tough, thick skinned, with a positive attitude and killer instinct. I believe this is nonsense. I've met incredible athletes, many have been among the most neurotic people I've ever come across; but when the time comes, despite their self-doubts they've been able to deliver. What you need is a strategy – a system that allows you to deal with your anxieties and doubts in a productive, positive way. I've developed such a system. It's taken years to tweak and adjust, but I know I can rely on it to deliver results, both for me and my clients.

I will describe the five areas where you need to excel if you want to become the best in the world. In cycling, when you become a world champion, as well as receiving a gold medal, you are presented with a cycling jersey. It's white with five horizontal bands. Running from top to bottom the bands are blue, red, black, yellow and green – the same colours as the Olympic rings – signifying the five continents. If you want to become world champion, you need to defeat athletes from all five continents. Winning the 'rainbow' jersey means you have the right to wear the stripes until the next world championships. Becoming a world champion isn't easy: to be a world champion you need to 'earn your stripes'.

The phrase is a military expression. As a soldier progresses through the ranks, he or she is awarded a higher level of insignia – a stripe. It takes time and hard work to earn your stripes, but you will reap the rewards. My Earn Your Stripes method involves five stripes; master these five areas and you will perform at a level you never thought possible. Even improving in one or two areas will let you operate at a higher level. Why not see how far you can go.

Stripe One: Drive

We start by looking at what drives and motivates *you*. Understanding this is crucial if you are to achieve your full potential. Drive isn't everything; if you are heading in the wrong direction, you'll never reach your intended destination. Make sure it's the direction you want. Drive and direction are a powerful combination.

Stripe Two: Performance

Next, we delve into performance, getting the most out of yourself through your working methods and choices. Planning and strategising are crucial, giving you confidence and conviction in your decisions. Most importantly, we look at redefining failure, seeing it as something to seek out and learn from.

Stripe Three: The team

There are no self-made winners: alongside every champion stands a team. In this section, we look at how you build a support network designed for success, using experts to optimise your performance. The environment around you will heavily influence how you approach challenges. If you create the right environment, filled with driven, talented people, your chances of achieving incredible things will be multiplied.

Stripe Four: Champion mindset

To be a champion, a champion mindset is required. Self-doubt, failures and self-sabotage are common:

champions find a way to push through. The human brain is an incredibly powerful tool, but it often tries to work against us. Subconsciously, a part of your brain tries to stop you progressing to new levels because it sees change as a threat. This section shows you how to fight back.

Stripe Five: Perform under pressure

The final section deals with performing under extreme pressure. The magnitude of a situation can often sabotage a performance. What if you could use the high-pressure situation to your advantage? This is where true champions excel.

If you master these Five Stripes you can achieve champion status. Earning your stripes takes time and effort, but the rewards are worth it. You can test your progress by completing the Earn Your Stripes scorecard at earn-your-stripes.co.uk. You receive a score for each Stripe, with suggestions on how to improve.

Nothing in this book is hard to learn or implement in isolation. It's all about creating habits and believing that what you are doing is the right thing. The first step is accepting responsibility for your own circumstances and performance. Some people feel the world has given them a rough deal; some simply get on with it and shape their own future. The American entrepreneur and author, Jim Rohn, said, 'It is the set of the sails, not the direction of the wind that determines which way we will go.'[1] If, deep down, you know you are capable of achieving more in your life, then please read on. If you simply enjoy books for the story, then welcome to the world of cycling.

Lastly, it would be easy to say, 'Well, it's alright for him, but I'm not a cyclist, so it doesn't apply to me.' My challenge is to think of similar situations in your own life and see how you can apply my method to them. I hope there are lessons to be learnt from all my stories.

1   Jim Rohn, Facebook, 21 August 2014, www.facebook.com
     /OfficialJimRohn/posts/it-is-the-set-of-the-sails-not-the-direction
     -of-the-wind-that-determines-which-w/10154462414660635

My Story

The high – London 2012

London has always seemed overwhelming. I love the pace and excitement, but after a day or two I usually feel the need to escape. People often talk about it being cold, and not just because of the all too familiar British weather. This time something was different. The city had come to life. People were smiling, they had something to talk about and through some incredible feat of planning, the sun was out. I had spent most of the past month glued to the television; my commute generally included several hundred refreshes of my social media feeds. I had caught the bug – Olympic fever.

I marvelled as the 'Queen' parachuted into the opening ceremony. I gaped in awe as Bradley Wiggins roared to victory on The Mall. Several times I leapt from my seat on Super Saturday. I even shed a tear as Katherine Grainger finally won that elusive gold medal.

Although I felt as much part of the Games as everyone else in 2012, I watched from a distance; first from Manchester and then from the training camp in Wales. I witnessed Chris Hoy, Jason Kenny, Laura Trott and Vicky Pendleton win medal after medal in 'The Pringle' – the velodrome in Stratford. These weren't just superheroes I was watching on my screen – they were my teammates. I felt excitement, fear, wonder; in just a matter of weeks it would be my turn. I would be competing in that very velodrome, on that very stage, in front of a passionate, noisy crowd. It would be my turn to go into battle.

As the Olympics drew to a close, I sensed a wave of sadness wash over London, as though the happiness, spirit and vibrancy people had experienced were coming to an end. Or were they? It was time to 'meet the superhumans', the Paralympic Games were coming to town. 'It's not something we've really seen much of before. Obviously, there's that Oscar Pistorius fellow, the blade runner.' Perhaps the less said about Oscar the better...

London was ready to give the Paralympics a go. Even if they proved half as good as the Olympics, it would be an incredible couple of weeks. After all, nobody wanted the wonderful atmosphere to end.

I arrived at the athletes' village a few days before the Games began. The village is an incredible place; I don't think there is anywhere more diverse on earth.

It's where the athletes and support staff stay prior to, during and after the Games. It is completely fenced off and closed to the public. This allows athletes to prepare for potentially the most important moment in their lives.

Up to ten thousand people stay in the village, and it has all the amenities you could expect. You can get your laundry done, spend time in the games and social rooms, use the gym and eat in the awe-inspiring food hall. The food hall can seat thousands of people at any one time and is enormous – the size of two football pitches. It serves food from across the globe, which can be both ideal and dangerous for competitors. A well-known burger bar in one corner can be an issue.

The day of the opening ceremony came. As my race was a couple of days away, it was decided that I shouldn't attend. The athletes have to stand for hours during the ceremony. The elation of being part of it is incredible, but the resulting fatigue can impact on performance. I watched it on TV with some of my teammates. We could see the stadium from the balcony of our apartment.

Something became immediately apparent; the people of London had bought into the Paralympic Games. The hype was immense, the Olympic Park in Stratford was packed, and the world's press had gathered. London's most incredible summer was set to continue. The festival of sport, joy and togetherness was to last another two weeks. Everyone could carry on enjoying themselves and the conversations, laughter and smiles on the Tube didn't have to stop. We were all in this together.

In contrast, I felt very alone that night. Most of the athletes had gone to bed before the end of the ceremony; sleep is crucial for performance. I shared a room with my tandem partner. Barney had been with the team a little longer than I, this was his third Paralympic Games as a tandem pilot. He was someone I looked to for guidance in the early days of my cycling career and was the most experienced tandem pilot in the world.

As usual, Barney fell asleep with ease. I found it more challenging. 'This is huge,' I thought to myself. 'I knew it would be big, but this is massive.' My mind was racing, I was going through all the possible permutations. 'What will happen if I win? All those years of hard work, working towards this moment, it all makes sense now. Think how proud my family will be. This is going to be live on TV, I could become a national icon, what will the celebrity life be like? Maybe I'll get invited onto *Question of Sport*.'

Then the flip side. 'What if I lose? I'm not favourite to win gold. My teammates are favourites, we're strong contenders, but maybe gold is a bit too much to ask. I'll be happy with any medal anyway.' My mind was racing, 'Training's been going so well though, I know we have a chance. What if I don't medal at all though? All those years of hard work for nothing. I'll be a nobody, worse than that, I'll be a failure.'

My heart pounded as I visualised my race in every detail. Sleeping seemed a long way off. I tossed and turned and eventually began to drift off. There was an almighty eruption of noise: bangs, blasts and a general shaking of the room. The noise caused me to leap out of bed in panic. London was under attack. My fight-or-flight response kicked in and I was ready to face the danger. Then it slowly dawned on me. The opening ceremony was coming to an end and the fireworks were right overhead. I got my breathing under control and looked to my left – Barney slept on.

The race

It was race day. Racing in the morning was a bit of a relief. It meant getting up early and forcing breakfast into a nervous stomach; having just one meal to worry about eating made life easier. Racing in the evening turns the day into an epic waiting game which can become a battle between your head and your body. You feel full of energy but know you must preserve it at all costs. There was no such issue on this occasion.

I arrived at the velodrome in plenty of time, over two hours before my race. All was quiet. A few mechanics from the different teams were working on their bikes while staff prepared the team areas. Fellow competitors appeared and started their warm-up routines. Announcements were made, the background music was turned up and spectators began to pour in through the doors.

The London velodrome, affectionately nicknamed the 'Pringle' on account of its roof resembling a popular, stackable crisp, allows for plenty of seating for spectators on either side of the track as the roof rises and curves sharply down in the middle. This means that if you are sitting at either end, you have a fantastic, unobstructed view of the track, but you can't see the spectators on the far side. The design means that the noise from the crowd is channelled down on to the track itself. When the crowd roars, you definitely know about it. Fortunately, I'd been to the velodrome the day before to sample the noise. I was standing in the middle of the arena next to Barney when a British rider was announced on track. The roar from the crowd was deafening, Barney turned to me and said something, but I couldn't hear a thing. We just looked at each other and laughed. This was a whole different level to anything we'd experienced before. I had no idea where my family was sitting, but I knew they'd be up there, watching, waiting, probably as nervous as me.

It was time to get on the bike and focus on getting myself ready. As I finished the warm-up on my static bike, I looked around. The stadium was full to capacity and the announcer was whipping the crowd into a frenzy. There were Union Flags everywhere. The excitement and expectation were palpable. But with expectation comes pressure.

The one-kilometre time trial, affectionately known as the 'kilo', is a timed event. Only one bike is on track at a time. The bikes are tandems with two riders: a visually impaired rider on the back and fully sighted rider on the front (the pilot). The tandem is mounted into a starting gate, which releases when the trackside count-down clock reaches zero. Once released from the gate, the riders accelerate the bike up to speed as quickly as possible. Each tandem is timed over a distance of one kilometre – four laps of the 250m velodrome. As only one bike is on track at a time, you can watch your rivals. The event is seeded, and as one of the favourites, Barney and I were one of the last bikes to go.

First out was a pair from Australia. On the back of the tandem was a legend of parasport, Kieran Modra. Kieran had achieved it all; this was his seventh Paralympic Games. He'd started out in athletics and swimming and had made the switch to cycling in Atlanta in 1996 where he had won the first of his gold medals. Just a couple of days before, he'd won gold in the four km pursuit. A gentle giant off the bike, he was a ferocious competitor on it. For obvious reasons, this was a man I looked up to. Sadly, Kieran was killed in a cycling accident in 2019. In my opinion, he was the greatest tandem stoker of all time. The Australian duo completed their effort in a time of 63.120 seconds, setting the benchmark for everyone else.

Feeling nervous is common on race day, but this wasn't just any old race day. My stomach was churning, and my mind was racing, 'What if I win, what if I lose?' Another competitor was announced on track, closely followed by an almighty roar from the crowd. The volume was incredible. I could feel the wave of noise hit me as they announced the pair from Argentina. I could only imagine how loud the crowd might be for us. The Argentinian pair burst out of the starting gate and within half a revolution of their pedals there was a loud bang. Their chain had come off. This is just one of the many things that can go wrong in tandem racing. 'What if that happens to us?' The stadium began to feel oppressive with the heat, noise and pressure. I looked at my watch, twenty minutes to go, time to visit the loo.

Never had I been so happy to be in a toilet; it was so quiet, so calm. 'I could stay here,' I thought to myself. 'Nobody would find me – at least not for a while. No, go, you need to get ready.' As I returned to track centre, I couldn't help but glance up at the crowd. 'Where's my family? What if I let them down? No, that's stupid, they will love you no matter what, Neil.'

The pair from Canada completed their ride. 'That's a solid time, I can beat that, though. It's OK.' I made my way back to my chair and put on my cycling shoes. Left foot first; always left foot first. Then I started pulling up the top half of my race skinsuit. Built to be aerodynamic, and not for comfort, this is one of those tasks that takes far more effort and sweating than you'd like. With the help of some of the British Cycling staff, I was able to squeeze myself in.

Five minutes to go. I picked up my helmet and gloves and began the walk to the chairs by the start line. 'Puff that chest out, Neil, some of your competitors might see you. Let them know who's boss,' I told myself. I sat down; the Spanish bike was ready to leave the starting gate. There was another pair of riders to my right. After them it would be my turn. I chose not to look at them, 'Just look straight ahead, Neil, and try to look calm.' My mind was racing, my stomach was churning and my mouth blisteringly dry. Outwardly, I tried to project a man at ease with his surroundings; I took a drink from my water bottle.

The Spanish pair posted an incredibly quick time to take the lead – 62.707 seconds – much quicker than we'd expected. 'OK, I'm going to have to do something special here.' The guys on my right made their way to the track. I became acutely aware of a TV camera pointing directly at me. 'Look cool, Neil, this is your track, look cool. I wish that bloody camera would go away!' The Dutch pair was flying round the track. Another roar from the crowd; they were in second place. Our turn next, 'Focus on the race, you know what you need to do. This is your time to shine.'

My coach and the squad mechanic carefully placed our bike into the starting gate. Barney and I made our way to the stairs leading up to the track side. Six steps to the most important moment of my life. Each step increased the weight on my shoulders. As I reached the top, I heard them announce, 'Representing Great Britain, Neil Fachie piloted by Barney Storey!' The noise from the crowd was deafening. I tried to look cool but all I could do was grin. 'This is incredible! Focus on the bike race, Neil.' I got on the bike and slowly strapped my feet into the pedals. I looked at the wooden track in front of me; the track that held the key to my future, to my destiny. I took a deep breath.

I looked at the countdown clock and realised that this was the last place I wanted to be. When it hit zero the bike would automatically release from the starting gate and I would be racing for Paralympic gold under the gaze of an expectant nation. The clock started ticking.

-15 seconds: 'Breathe, Neil, all the training has been for this moment, you can do this. I don't want to be here. Yes, you do. This is your moment.'

-10 seconds: 'OK, no going back now, keep breathing.'

-5 seconds: 'Focus now.'

-4 seconds: 'Think about the start.'

-3 seconds: 'You can do this.'

-2 seconds: 'My heart's beating so fast.'

-1 second: 'Breathe in.'

Having watched the footage, I can describe how the ride played out. At the time, however, the first three laps (of four) were a blur. In a race, your mind empties and you run on autopilot. Blood rushes to your muscles so they have the oxygen they need to perform to their maximum. The one-kilometre time trial is an extremely physically demanding event. At maximal effort for about sixty seconds, the legs produce a huge amount of lactic acid. This causes them to become less effective as the race progresses. It means that the bike that decelerates the least, or in other words, copes best with the lactic acid build-up, is the one that ultimately wins the race.

At the start of the final lap – the point at which the pain really starts to hit – I suddenly became aware again. We were 0.726 of a second ahead of the Spanish pair (though I had no idea of this at the time); head down, I was pushing as hard as I could on the pedals. I could hear something garbled from the announcer, followed by another huge roar. I knew the crowd was willing us on; they had come to see success for Great Britain, and I knew I had to deliver. I found something within myself that I'd never found before. A feeling of strength, an ability to dig deeper than I thought possible. I pushed as hard as I could, willing the finish line to come more quickly. The lap flashed by and we crossed the finish line. In that final lap we'd almost doubled our lead over the bike from Spain, taking a further 0.630 seconds off them. The announcer said something I couldn't make out, and then three words that were as clear as day: 'New world record.'

What followed was one of the finest displays of over-the-top celebration. Although I have very little rec-ollection of it, I've watched it back and I milked the moment. Pumping my fists in the air, I waved at the crowd and finished up with what looks like the Usain Bolt 'lightning bolt' pose. This was my moment; I was a Paralympic Champion.

Aftermath

Becoming a Paralympic Champion was only something I'd dreamed about in recent years, as a child it had never been on my radar. There I was, in the centre of the velodrome in London, about to take the top place on the podium. 'Winners of the gold medal, represent-ing Great Britain and Northern Ireland, Neil Fachie piloted by Barney Storey.' Cue deafening roar; cue inane grin. I'd won a few medals during my sporting career, but nothing prepared me for the moment that giant, weighty gong was placed around my neck. When you wore this medal, you knew you'd made it big. After I received the flowers, I raised my hand to the watch-ing crowd, another huge roar and thousands of flags. 'Ladies and Gentlemen, please stand for the national anthem of Great Britain.' I didn't dare sing – something I'd later be criticised for on social media. I do not have the voice of an angel and I was afraid that the cameras and microphone would pick me up cracking under the weight of the emotion; I'd seen (and heard) it happen to lots of footballers and rugby players in the line-up before an international match.

Luckily, the stadium sang for me, almost 7,000 people singing with pride; the venue was a magical place to be that morning. A huge roar went up at the end and we held our arms aloft. In that moment I felt as though I had so much power. I'd turn to one side of the crowd and wave, they'd roar; I'd turn to the other side, same again. Surreal doesn't come close; for this brief moment in time, we were superstars.

Press interviews and photos followed. The click, click, click from the wall of photographers was incessant. 'Over here, Neil.' 'Neil, look down here.' 'Bite the medal!' I hate this weird tradition. I don't make a habit of chewing on metal, and even if I did, I definitely wouldn't be chomping down on this beauty. Draped in the Union Flag, we posed for what seemed like a lifetime. My face started to ache from smiling. As a typical dour Scotsman, I don't make a habit of smiling; I'd done very little training for it. A member of our press team asked, 'Where do you want your golden pillar box to be, Neil?' 'My what?' This hadn't even crossed my mind. 'Oh, and by the way, you're going to be on a stamp tomorrow.'

All this madness came to an end when a man came over to inform me that I had been asked to visit anti-doping. The next hour was spent in a windowless room beneath the stands, waiting until I was hydrated enough to wee into a cup. Elite sport is certainly not all glamour! Every few minutes I would look at my gold medal and smile. Having duly filled a plastic cup with pee, it was back to the village to rest and refuel.

The following day we competed in the sprint event. This involves a whole day of racing. First a qualifying ride against the clock – the flying 200m. Basically, you have a few laps to build up your speed, before riding as fast as possible over a distance of 200 m. The fastest time qualifies in position number one, the second fastest in position two and so on. Despite my aching legs from the previous day, we managed to qualify in second place, behind our British teammates. What follows is a series of races in the quarters, semis and finals. Two bikes race and whoever crosses the line first wins; each round is a best of three rides. It's a highly tactical race and it often pays to keep behind your opponents, forcing them to do all the hard work, while you sit in their slipstream, ready to pounce at the end.

The sight of two tandems hurtling round the track at full speed is incredible; the spectators love it and I adore it. Nothing matches the adrenaline rush of battling against two other guys who are determined to pip you at the finish line, travelling at speeds in excess of 70 kph. We comfortably defeated the Argentinian pair two rides to nil in the quarterfinals, before defeating the Spanish duo two nil in the semis. The final was against the other British tandem, ridden by Anthony Kappes and Craig Maclean. It was a hard-fought battle, but ultimately, they were too strong for us. Their gold medal made up for the previous day's disappointment that was a result of a mechanical issue.

We backed up our gold medal success with silver in the sprint; I was happy with what we had achieved. After the ceremony, and with another large medal around my neck, we were asked to collect our things. Then followed probably the most surreal experience in my career. The four of us hopped on the back of a buggy driven through the Olympic Park. As we were driven past crowds either waiting to enter venues, leaving venues or watching events on the large screens, I realised just how massive the Paralympic Games were. People were shouting, pointing, waving and cheering at us. They knew exactly who we were, and we were treated as celebrities. As we got off the buggy at the media area, a little girl approached me. 'Is this you?' I looked down at the playing card she was holding out with my face and name on it. 'Yeah, weird.' She offered to give it to me, but I told her to keep it. I certainly didn't need to look at my face and I didn't want to remove a card from her pack.

Within minutes we were taken on to the studio floor of Channel 4's temporary studios, appearing live on the sofa. This was my first experience of live studio television and it was daunting having several cameras pointing at you. I have no recollection of the interview at all – either it went without a hitch or I've blocked it from my memory for my own psychological well-being. After the show, we were taken to Great Britain House for radio interviews and, more importantly, champagne. GB House is a place for athletes to meet up with their families and friends during the Games. As you need accreditation to get in, it is a sanctuary outside of the village. Having seen the madness of the Olympic Park and how recognisable we were, I was relieved to be somewhere a little calmer after two days of hard racing.

After all the endless TV and radio interviews, I had some time to myself. I stood, champagne in hand, trying to take it all in. My phone was buzzing with notifications and updates. I was a Paralympic Champion, but what did that even mean? The alcohol from the bubbles worked its way into my system, one that had been alcohol free for months. It felt good to be with other athletes who'd had the same experience and try to make sense of it all. It had taken years of hard work, years of battling against the doubters, years of battling against self-doubt. Now I felt like a somebody. My plan to reach the top had been completed successfully.

As I relaxed and began to take in the magnitude of it all, the madness began again. We appeared on a small stage in front of friends and family and were interviewed about our experience. As we left the stage to take our seats, Tony Hadley was introduced. He burst into the room, belting out a rendition of Spandau Ballet's cult classic 'Gold'. I have no idea how many times he must have sung that song during the Games, but thanks to my alcohol-induced, relaxed state, this time I was perfectly happy to sing along.

For the next week or so we were rock stars. Whenever I ventured outside the village into the Olympic Park, I quickly learnt that attempting to get anywhere wearing the GB kit was impossible. Once one person spotted you and asked for an autograph, you were instantly surrounded by swarms of people. Don't get me wrong, I loved it, but it meant meeting up with friends became a challenge.

On one trip to an event, we were flanked by security. They formed a perimeter around us and shepherded us through the crowds. I've never felt so rock 'n' roll. We got up on the stage to show our medals to an enthusiastic crowd. Understandably, it was hard to wipe the grin off my face. Other appearances around London meant I had a busy week. Life was pretty special.

After the Paralympic Games ended there was one last hurrah. The athletes' parade through the streets of London. The Paralympic GB team was joined by the Olympic GB team. We stood together as one team on floats that wended their way through the city. Around one million people came to see us, and it was mind-blowing. Crowds lined the whole route from

Mansion House in the City to Trafalgar Square. In places they were twenty to thirty deep. I've never done so much waving or smiling and it was a fitting end to an incredible couple of months for London.

Often a low follows an immense high. I did find normality a struggle for a while, but I was kept very busy. There was a flood of requests to appear at schools and at events and, given I was taking time off from training, I tried to do as much as I could. There were numerous ceremonies to attend and awards to collect. There were parades in Glasgow and Aberdeen, which meant a chance to visit my gold postbox. Rather fittingly, it's located in Golden Square in Aberdeen, on the corner with Silver Street. Almost as though it was meant to be.

The accolades kept coming – Aberdeen Sports Person of the Year, Scottish Disability Sports Person of the Year, among others. I received an honorary doctorate from the University of Aberdeen and – the pinnacle – I was awarded an MBE for services to cycling in the 2013 New Year Honours List. All this for riding a bicycle round and round in circles.

I took some time to reflect and look back on my journey. Although there had been a lot of struggles, never in my wildest dreams did I imagine that I would find myself in this position. For years I had fought and clawed my way forward, often feeling that I was never getting anywhere. My ambition had been simply to make it to London 2012. How had it gone so right for once?

It became clear that it was my shift in focus when I joined British Cycling that had made a significant impact. What I had done previously had given me the drive and direction, British Cycling gave me the tools and support network, the rest was down to hard work and perseverance.

The low – Beijing 2008

Back in 2008, just four years earlier, life looked completely different. I had graduated from university in 2006 and become a full-time athlete. But not in cycling; my first love had been athletics. In fact, this is what I had dedicated much of my teenage life to. In 2006 my hobby became my career, and in 2008 I became a Paralympian.

At that stage, simply qualifying for the Games was a huge achievement. Being a realist, I was aware that the chance of a medal was slim at best, but I had hopes that something magical might happen when I got there. Perhaps just being at the Paralympics would boost my performance, elevating me to medal contender, perhaps even winner.

Before we went to Beijing, I received my team kit-bag. I took huge delight in trying on every item of the ParalympicsGB-branded clothing: T-shirts, shorts, trainers, socks, suit, parade wear, hats and even sunglasses. It was like an immensely patriotic Christmas

Day. Even more bizarrely, it was when I was watching Usain Bolt light up the track at the Beijing Olympics on TV. He was breaking world records on the very track I would be running on in just a few weeks.

Before Beijing, I spent a few days on the coastal islands of Macau – the Vegas of Asia. No gambling for me however, just training and adjusting to the climate and time zone. It was the holding camp for ParalympicsGB prior to the Games and an opportunity for the team to come together in an environment conducive to success.

There were athletes from multiple sports, some first timers like me and those who had been there and done it before. Experienced individuals full of confidence and purpose. The team was in high spirits and I was excited. I was globe-trotting, training in sunshine and generally being looked after. Soon I'd be able to call myself a Paralympian.

I arrived at Beijing Airport, my first time in China, and made my way to the Paralympic desk at Arrivals. Paralympic and Games logos were everywhere. We were whisked off in a coach to the Athletes' Village. The entire route was lined with Paralympic Games flags and it was clear that China was making a big deal of it.

As we pulled up to the entrance gates, I was surprised at the level of security. It never occurred to me that we were the kind of people who needed to be protected. Did it mean I was a celebrity of some sort? Men with semi-automatic weapons smiled at us and I smiled back; best not make them angry.

Eyes wide and jaw agape I wandered through the village. Giant national flags were draped from balconies and roofs of the apartment blocks. There were shops, a gym, hairdressers, buses and people from across the globe. The vast food hall had row-upon-row of canteen-style tables and chairs as far as the eye could see. The far wall was lined with buffet-style cuisine from around the world. I didn't even know where to start.

Our apartment wasn't particularly luxurious. It had three bedrooms, each housing two athletes, and a small living space. From our small balcony, I could see the laundry centre below and the games room opposite. This was where athletes could go to relax and unwind. There was even a computer room with Wi-Fi access. If I sat on my balcony I could just about pick up a signal. This was home for the next couple of weeks. I had made it.

The following day we were at the warm-up track next to the iconic Bird's Nest Stadium, a ninety-thousand seater where I would be competing. I managed to sneak in a walk down the tunnel and into the stadium. This was where Usain Bolt had blown the opposition away and where the opening ceremony would take place. They were rehearsing for the opening ceremony, a closely guarded secret – it was only a few seconds before a steward ran over to usher me out.

The ceremony was incredible, I marched in with the team filled with excitement and pride. I had never been in a stadium as big as this before. We took our seats and watched the rest of the incredible displays, listened to the speeches and most magical of all, watched the Paralympic Flame being lit. Not only was I a little emotional, I had fallen in love with the Paralympics. It was an experience I didn't want to end.

My race days were slightly anti-climactic. My heat for the 100m was in the morning. Everything went to plan, despite my nerves. When I walked into the stadium, I was disappointed to see there were only about thirty-thousand people. It hadn't occurred to me that the stadium might not be full for the morning session.

We were called to our starting blocks and I went through my routine. Walk forward over the starting blocks, two jumps on the spot, slap my thighs and drop down into my starting position; take a deep breath, look down the track and then drop my gaze to the starting line. I made a blistering start – always my strong point – and took an early lead. As I came out of my drive phase I became aware of competitors overtaking. I gradually slipped down the order and crossed the line in fifth place. I wouldn't be racing in the final. My time wasn't particularly fast; the magic of the Games hadn't struck. I was distinctly average. I went to the track the following evening to watch the final of my event. Sure enough, the stadium was packed and rather than taking part, I was just an onlooker. Never mind, I had another chance in the 200m. I considered this to be my stronger event.

As with the 100m, my 200m heat was in the morning and again a relatively quiet stadium greeted me as I approached the start line. I went through the same ritual; this time there was a false start by the Brazilian athlete. I'd raced this guy before and half of the time he would be disqualified for two false starts. We got back on our marks and the gun went, again another false start. Sure enough, the Brazilian was disqualified. Third time lucky. My Paralympic 200-metre career had finally got underway – and then ended. As with the 100m, I was very average. Again, I was placed ninth overall, one place away from making the final. Again, I would have to watch it from the stand.

Despite two disappointing performances, the Games had awoken something in me. I was a Paralympian; nobody could ever take that away from me. I had achieved something incredible. Although I was proud of myself, I wanted more. I had fallen in love with the Paralympic Games and being surrounded by incredible people. Many of them had experienced something life-changing, or, like me, had been born with a condition that required approaching the world in a different way. I was fascinated. Then there was the Games themselves. I had never appreciated how huge they were. A ninety-thousand seat stadium filled every night, this was the real deal.

Coming from an environment where I usually trained on my own in Aberdeen, I craved being part of a team. ParalympicsGB filled that void and I met some amazing people. I dreaded going home, back to a life where my school and university friends were working nine-to-five. However, I knew there was a brilliant, bright ray of hope on the horizon. In four years' time, the Games would take place again. Unbelievably, they would be in London. A home Paralympic Games – not many people are lucky enough to experience that.

I knew I would have to make a few changes. If I was to keep going for another four years, I would need to re-evaluate my approach. I had only just scraped into the team for these Games, if I was to guarantee myself a place in London in four years, I would have to step up to the next level. Wouldn't it be incredible to make the final in London? Imagine running in front of a huge home crowd, an experience that would stick with me forever. I was excited; it was a new dawn, a time to shine.

Back to reality

After a long flight, I arrived back in Aberdeen. The anti-climax hit me immediately. I knew it was unlikely, but I imagined a hero's welcome. Instead, I trudged through a quiet airport and into the cold air of northeast Scotland. My best friend had offered to pick me up, so at least I could chat to him before he had to go to work.

The house was empty – my family still had a few more days in China. While they were having a fantastic time, visiting landmarks like the Great Wall and Tiananmen Square, I was faced with a mountain of washing. After weeks of being surrounded by teammates, I found myself alone. I had heard about the 'post-Games blues', but I wasn't prepared for how instant and hard-hitting they would be. My coach advised me to stay away from training for a few weeks, I needed time off. As I didn't have anything else in my life, I felt very empty; but the lure of London 2012 was still there.

After a week or two, I received a phone call from a member of British Athletics. Before working with them, I'd been informed that they were straight talking. They definitely took no prisoners. The call was brief and I can't remember it word for word, but this is what has stayed with me, 'We've had our review meeting and we've come to the decision that we don't feel you have the potential to make it to London 2012. As such we are removing you from the programme – effective immediately.'

I tried to argue my case, but the decision had been made. I was utterly devastated. I was also very angry. I felt it was their fault that I hadn't performed to my best. They had expected too much of me, they couldn't see the big picture, they hadn't done their jobs out in Beijing properly. I blamed everyone, my coach, my support team. Why weren't they doing everything they could for me?

I spoke to someone from my local Institute of Sport who had supported me up to then. They were willing to continue providing physiotherapy and strength and conditioning support in the short-term. Otherwise I would have to fend for myself. British Athletics had cut the small amount of funding I was receiving, and I couldn't afford to continue as a full-time athlete – the dream was over.

I started applying for jobs: secretarial jobs, a disability support officer at the university, a data analyst with the police force. I needed to find work, move on with my life and put all of this behind me. I found filling in the application forms utterly soul destroying. This wasn't how I had imagined life after the Paralympics. The rejection letters started arriving. You're over-qualified, you don't have enough experience, there was very strong competition for the role. The same old excuses again and again. I was a Paralympian, I was a Physics graduate, I was a nobody.

Between job applications I was on my Xbox. I had always been a bit of a video gaming addict, but now I had all the time in the world. There was nothing better than being in a different world, living a life that wasn't mine. One with goals, purpose and direction. The lure of one more challenge, one more match or one more fight was too great. I easily spent ten hours a day playing games. I was shutting myself off from the real world, one I didn't want to be part of.

My diet began to suffer. I started eating things that made me happy. The kind of food, that if I was training full-time, I could have just about got away with. I was eating more chocolate, more chips and discovered a new favourite, nachos! Well, my take on nachos; grab some crisps, grate some cheese, whack it in the microwave and you're good to go. It only took a couple of minutes and was the perfect snack before another session on the Xbox. Understandably, I started putting on weight, something I'd never had to deal with. I had always taken a great deal of pride in my physique as an athlete. Because of my sport, I'd always assumed I was one of those people who could get away with eating whatever they liked. Apparently not.

Between gaming marathons, I'd make the weekly trip to sign on at the job centre and fill out their many forms. At least it got me outside. I know many people have gone through this process and will understand how degrading it can feel: 'How many jobs have you applied for this week?', 'What responses have you had?', 'What jobs would you like to do?', 'How does your disability affect your ability to work?'

'Well – I can't drive to work, so it would need to be something I can get to by public transport. I would need a bigger screen and something to help magnify any paper documents I need to read.'

And the question that really got me, 'Was my disability affecting my job prospects?'

I started ticking the box on application forms under the guaranteed interview scheme. This ensures that a person with a disability is not discriminated against at the point of submitting their application form. It meant I couldn't be turned down until they had spoken to me face-to-face. I soon became aware that at each interview, I was asked the same question, 'How will your disability affect your ability to do the job?' Even when I pointed out that there was funding to cover any special equipment I might need, businesses were still reluctant to consider me. The standard responses came in, 'There was a lot of competition for the role, we just didn't think you were the right fit.' I had a flashback to a careers' day at university. I approached the guy from the RAF and explained my situation. I asked if there were any roles in the RAF I could do with a visual impairment. Without hesitation he said, 'No'. Although I pointed out I had no intention of flying planes, he still replied with a point-blank no. It was beginning to add up. My disability was an issue to employers, whether they admitted it or not.

Despite the fact I had successfully worked my way through school, obtained a degree in physics and made it to the Paralympics, I was seemingly not suitable for employment. My eye condition was defeating me, and I felt as though my education had been for nothing. Unfit, overweight, on the dole, living at home, no prospects and no hope.

I slipped into depression. I spent most of my time on my own in the house. Human interaction was minimal, bar the occasional chat on Messenger and a weekly poker night with my best friends. I craved those nights, but as soon as everyone left, I was back in my grey world.

I wasn't particularly sad; I was just numb. I didn't get upset. Any feeling I did show was anger. If something went wrong in a video game, I'd shout at the screen and throw the control pad across the room. I knew it wasn't the game I was angry at, but it felt good to release some emotion. I was short with my parents who were doing their best for me and providing me with food and shelter at no cost. I couldn't have been luckier, but I wasn't grateful.

I felt as though I had no purpose. I couldn't see a path I wanted to take. Unlike in the games I was playing, I had no clear objective, there was no tutorial to show me how to act and I didn't possess superhuman abilities. I had been single for a year and a half and was still bitter about the break up. I wasn't meeting anyone new and, frankly, I was too embarrassed about my appearance and current situation to put myself out there. I had never exactly been a ladies' man; I was too self-conscious to brave talking to girls I'd never met.

As my situation got worse, self-consciousness moved to self-loathing. I was resentful of who I was, and I resented my disability. I felt as though the world had let me down. My solution was to go deeper into the world of gaming, claim job seeker's allowance and live a life of solitude. The year had promised so much and, in many respects, delivered: I was a Paralympian and had been to Beijing. But here I was: disabled, disinterested and disheartened: 2008 wasn't turning out the way I had in mind.

The spark

Between long bouts of numbness and days of gaming, there were flashes of insight. I can't pinpoint the exact moment, but one morning in late 2008 I woke up and something had shifted. Ideas were pinging around my head. Little flashbulbs firing somewhere in my brain; I felt alive for the first time in weeks.

During my time in British Athletics, the Olympic and Paralympic teams had to undergo standard fitness and strength-based assessments. I had excelled at some of these tests, scoring higher than the whole of both squads. If I was physically that strong, why had I never been able to run faster? Was there something I was doing wrong? Should I completely rebuild myself as an athlete or try a new event? Is athletics even the right sport for me?

During the Beijing Paralympics, Liz Mendl, a fellow Scot who was working for the British Paralympic Association and sportscotland, had mentioned something. Although I had laughed it off at the time, it was now piquing my interest. She'd said, 'I think you'd be pretty handy on the back of a tandem.' What if there was another sport out there for me? I had dedicated my sporting life to athletics since the age of ten, why had I assumed it was the sport I would be best at? Ever since I got that fateful call from my manager at British Athletics, telling me they were letting me go, I'd assumed that was the end for me. There was no way back. It felt as though they were closing the door on my Paralympic dreams. What if there was another way in?

I had a number of options. I could continue with athletics, trying to fight my way back into the team. I could experiment with different events – maybe stepping up to 400m. It didn't seem like the best option. I had been doing athletics for over half of my life and it felt like I had reached my potential. It would take an incredible effort just to return to the shape I was in at Beijing. It seemed unlikely that any amount of hard work would get me to the level of medal contender.

Another option would be to try something new. I had nothing to lose. I was at my lowest point, so what did it matter if I tried something and failed. I couldn't be any further from the London Paralympic Games than I was now. London 2012 was where I wanted to be, the thought of sitting at home and watching it on TV filled me with dread. I doubted I would even be able to handle it. I knew how much the Paralympics meant to me and to represent ParalympicsGB in my own country was my holy grail. This was too big a dream to give up on. Lots could happen in four years – I could learn a new sport.

I felt the adrenaline pumping through my body – a feeling I recognised from my sporting days. It felt as though I was standing on the start line, about to push my body to the limit and do battle with my rivals. My muscles twitched; my heart rate quickened. I leapt out of bed, raced to the loo, made a cup of tea (priorities) and sat at my computer.

It took some time to research each of the Paralympic sports and establish which ones were for people with a visual impairment. Trying each one out was going to take a whole lot longer. I had absolute clarity: my goal was to make the ParalympicsGB team for London 2012. I would have to find the right sport to show enough potential in. I would put everything into making the team. If I failed, so be it, at least I could watch the Games without wondering 'what if?'

I have loved cycling since I was a child. Growing up, my eyesight was still good enough to let me hop on my bike and cycle round the neighbourhood. The roads weren't too busy and there were plenty of great off-road rides in the woods and moorlands near my house. I loved the feeling of speed and freedom it gave me. My friends hated going out with me, though, as I would insist on racing everywhere or challenge them to bigger jumps or trickier downhill descents. It's safe to say that I've always been competitive.

I didn't just love riding my bike, I remember watching Greg LeMond ride to victory in the 1990 Tour de

France for Team Z. I marvelled at the bunch sprints and mountain climbs. Something always made me nervous, though; the guys always took their hands off the handlebars, raising their arms to celebrate if they won a stage. I couldn't do that. What kind of cyclist would I be if I won a race and didn't do a 'no-hands' celebration? After each of the Tour de France stages, I'd spend hours cycling up and down my street practising and building up confidence. I'd visualise myself sprinting to the line and crossing it ahead of my rivals. I'd raise my arms high and punch the air – a real cyclist. I can only imagine what the neighbours thought.

I looked at my list of possible sports for London 2012. At the top was cycling; it was time to commit. I knew from my physique that if I was going to succeed, it would be as a track sprinter – I would have to ride the velodrome.

I found the phone number for Manchester Velodrome. I've always been incredibly nervous of phone calls, usually persuading my mum to make them for me. I took a deep breath, typed in the number, pressed call and waited.

'National Cycling Centre, how can I help?'

'Erm, I would like to try riding on the velodrome, is that possible?'

'Yes, love, taster sessions run most days, it costs £16 and that includes bike and helmet hire. Next available session is Wednesday at 1pm, does that suit you?'

'Err, yeah.'

'OK, love, do you know what frame size you are?'

'Frame size?'

'How tall are you?'

'Five foot two roughly.'

'How old did you say you are?'

'Twenty-four.'

'Alright, love, I just need your card details and we'll see you next week.'

Right, that happened fast. Should I have mentioned that I can't see very well? Probably. Ah well, too late now and they might not have let me have a go.

I went to Manchester the following week, the seven-hour train journey meant I couldn't do it in one day, so I stayed with a friend. I arrived at the velodrome reception, collected my bike and helmet and headed into the track centre. I instantly regretted my decision. The track looked really cool on TV – similar to an athletics track but shorter at 250m – made of wood with bankings on each turn. These bankings were ginormous, about three metres high. Apparently, I was meant to ride round this. Surely a lot of people died on taster sessions. Fortunately, the coach was on hand to offer some reassuring advice. 'If you go too slow, stop pedalling, or turn the bars too sharply, you will fall off.' 'Right you are.' I thought, 'Should I have told him I can't see very well? Too late now...'

I gripped the bars for dear life, my muscles so tense that I began to shake. Keeping well away from everyone else, I wobbled my way around the base of the track on my hire bike, with its skinny tyres and lack of brakes. As I completed a lap, I heard the coach bellowing, 'Faster, faster, you need to go faster.' Slowly my confidence grew, and I started riding further and further up the track, until I reached halfway up the wall of death at each end. As I began to relax, I experienced that sense of speed and freedom that I had loved so much as a child. I felt alive.

I survived my first track cycling experience and loved it. After the session I got chatting to a guy. He'd spotted my Beijing Paralympics bag and called me over. His name was Craig Maclean. I recognised Craig, I'd watched him ride to silver in the team sprint at the Sydney Olympics in 2000 with Chris Hoy and Jason Queally. And again, at the Commonwealth Games in 2006 with Chris and Ross Edgar when they had won gold for Scotland. He was warming up for the GB

Cycling Team session that was about to take place. He told me that he had just transferred from the Olympic Team to the Paralympic Team. He was now what was known as a 'pilot', a fully sighted person who rides on the front of a tandem, with a visually impaired rider on the back. He was struggling to find a talented visually impaired athlete to ride with, did I know anyone? Some things are just meant to be.

There I was, at my lowest ebb, sitting in front of my Xbox, with weekly trips to the job centre. I had no direction. The bright spark of hope of competing at the London 2012 Paralympics had been temporarily extinguished. I had no reason or desire to do anything about it, and on those rare occasions when I felt slightly motivated, my first thought would be, 'Where do I even start?' That morning in late 2008, I decided to stop feeling sorry for myself and take action. After months of soul searching, I knew what I wanted from life. Getting to the London 2012 Paralympic Games was my drive. Although the prospect of chasing this dream scared me, it also made me feel alive. I knew from experience that if I was serious, I needed to make some radical changes in my approach. Simply going with the flow was no longer an option; I needed to make it happen. I needed to learn to strategise, execute and be relentless in my pursuit of this goal.

Without realising it, that morning I created my first version of the Earn Your Stripes methodology. Since then it has been adapted, refined and perfected. It's a system that has taken me from unemployed, overweight and depressed in late 2008, to Paralympic Champion at London 2012. Its longevity has meant that I've continued to progress and develop, extending my sporting career to well over a decade. The system continues to shape my sporting career, as well as my business career, and has contributed to the success of my clients. As I mentioned in the Introduction, it consists of five key areas, the first of which is Drive. Without having the drive and motivation to make the ParalympicsGB squad for London, none of this would have happened for me. It's time to discover what drives you. It's time to find out how to Earn Your Stripes.

Stripe One: Drive

If there is one thing I've learnt in life, it's that people generally aren't willing to put a whole lot of effort into doing something they don't really believe in. I came very close to writing 'time and effort', but that's not strictly true. Many people seem to spend an inordinate amount of time doing things they neither enjoy nor believe in. This is because of the belief that our purpose as good citizens is to work through the school system, before moving on to a trade, college or university. From there it's forty-five years or so of hard work, saving up to enjoy the fruits of our labour in retirement. The system is designed to get the most out of you, but are you getting the most out of yourself? Are you living the life that you want? The life that the child in you envisaged. If not, what's stopping you?

Finding the thing that drives you can be a challenge. Busy lives and social norms get in the way, keeping you locked in the status quo. But like all challenges, there is a way to overcome it. I've created a tool to help you earn the first of the five stripes – drive. DRIVE is the acronym for my simple five-step process that helps you find what truly motivates you:

Disrupt

Reflect

Invite opportunities

Vision

Energy

Disrupt

I believe that to make changes, you first need to disrupt your normal pattern of thinking and behaving. In my experience, both in my own career and that of the clients I coach, most of us have been worn down over the years. Our youthful approach to life has disappeared. We no longer look at the world with wonder, imagining what the future might hold. Once we are comfortably settled in employment, our concerns gradually shift towards smaller things: paying the bills, what our next meal should be and what to watch on TV.

There's no shame in this, being comfortable isn't a bad thing, but it does reduce the chances of leading a more fulfilled, successful life that our younger selves dreamed of. When I was at my lowest point, rather than continuing down the route I had been on – playing Xbox, applying for jobs and generally shutting off from the world – I decided to turn things upside down. That morning in late 2008, I decided to disrupt my normal routine and mindset. It's the process of breaking the mould and daring to dream. In order to find your drive, you first need a spark. London 2012 was the spark I needed to make that change, but there have been others. Each spark has created an inflexion point on my journey, after which massive change has taken place.

As humans, we often feel the need to challenge ourselves, constantly making improvements along the way. Despite these improvements, one thing does seem to deteriorate over time – our ability to dream. I remember many would-be footballers, movie stars and rulers of the world in my class at school.

So, what happens? Along the way we temper our expectations. The world doesn't always treat us well and people are quick to tell us not to set our sights too high; we need to be realistic. What most people define as realism is actually a gross underestimation of ability. You are capable of great things; you just haven't learnt the process to achieve them.

My first notable disrupt moment came during the summer of 2005. I had just completed the third year of my four-year physics degree at the University of Aberdeen. I was beginning to find the degree a struggle and couldn't really foresee myself pursuing physics as a career. 'You have to get through this final year and then hopefully find work,' I regularly told myself. Meanwhile, I was a committed athlete and training five days a week took up most of my free time. Despite being visually impaired and a keen sportsperson, it wasn't until that summer that I became aware of para-sport. I had always assumed my eyesight was too good to be considered a disabled athlete, but this was probably more down to denial of my disability.

While I was watching athletics on television, I noticed a race for elite athletes with a disability. This sparked my interest. Was this something I could get involved in? This led to a series of emails and phone calls to Scottish Disability Sport and British Athletics. In late 2005, I was given the opportunity I'd been looking for. I was invited to a training day with the British Athletics Paralympic Development Squad. I jumped at the chance. There was talk of World Championships and Paralympic Games among the team. Far from any quelling of dreams, they were encouraged. I was immediately hooked; this was a path I wanted to take.

I was offered a place on the development programme, with a small amount of funding through the National Lottery to cover some of my expenses. After a series of eye tests, I was told I would be competing in the T13 class. This is a category for athletes with a visual impairment. To be eligible to compete, the athlete must have, after correction, less than 10% vision of a fully sighted person.

In April 2006, I was selected to compete at my first World Championships taking place later that summer in the Netherlands. The effort I had to put in meant my final exams at university suffered. Somehow, I managed to get a 2:2 and I was free to focus fully on what I loved; I became a full-time athlete. It was obvious to see the difference in performance between my educational and sporting exploits. A clear indication that I perform much better when I have bought into the overall goal.

The next big moment was when I received my kit for the championships. I lifted the British running vest from the box. I'd seen so many great athletes compete in this over the years, now I had my own. When I was growing up, I'd idolised athletes such as Linford Christie, Colin Jackson, John Regis, Roger Black and Iwan Thomas. I felt I was joining their ranks. All my T-shirts, tracksuits and tops had Great Britain emblazoned across them. I would be representing my country; I wondered what it would feel like to step on to that track.

Summer 2006 was pretty special. Travelling with the British Athletics team to the World Championships was an eye opener. Elite athletes at the top of their game train hard and follow a lifestyle designed to get results. If I was going to become a World Champion, I had a lot to learn. Competing in the 100m and 200m races, I performed well. I made both finals, finishing sixth in the 200m and seventh in the 100m. A solid start in international competition, although I was still some way off from the medals. This was the start of a journey with many ups and downs, but with an end goal. I wanted to be a World Champion, I wanted to be a Paralympic Champion and spend my time doing something that excited me. Ultimately, though, was the desire to prove to the world, and myself, what I and the wider community of people with a disability are capable of.

By disrupting my normal pattern of thinking, I had awakened new possibilities. I began to dream about competing on a global stage. I could see myself sprinting to glory. Visualising this dream gave me excitement, passion and, most importantly, momentum. Without something to aim for, it's much harder to motivate yourself.

Does this ring true with you? Have you ever found yourself in a similar situation where you were simply going through the motions? Maybe it's time to disrupt the status quo and consider what you might be capable of.

TAKE ACTION

Take the opportunity to unleash your inner child. Dare to dream and don't feel restricted by so-called reality.

Answer these questions:

- Are you satisfied with your current situation?
- Where would you like to see yourself in three, five- or ten-years' time?

Once you've come up with an answer, dream it. Picture what that scenario looks and feels like to you. How would your life be different? Visualisation is something we explore in more detail later on, but it can be an immensely powerful tool. I don't buy in to simply, 'If you dream it, you can be it'. But if you can dream it, you can create a spark. Disrupt your thought process, create the image, find that spark and hold on to it. You're going to need it.

Reflect

Once we've broken the status quo by disrupting our normal thought patterns, it's time to move on to phase two of DRIVE – Reflect. This means spending time thinking about where you are and where you've been. It is an opportunity to evaluate what makes you tick. Self-reflection is something most of us think we do, but in reality, we never actually take the time to clear everything else away to properly think.

Following the disappointment of losing my funding from British Athletics in 2008, I had ample opportunity to reflect on my life. My options were: I could continue to be unemployed and living off benefits, I could find a suitable job and put in the hours, or I could take a risk and chase a dream. The third option very much felt like a gamble, everyone else was getting jobs and progressing in the expected way. I had practically no money to my name, so pursuing full-time sport with no funding seemed foolhardy. Inevitably, many people advised me to pick a more normal route. What they didn't realise was that having spent time reflecting on my journey, I knew what would suit me best.

At the age of four, I was diagnosed with a congenital eye condition known as Retinitis Pigmentosa (RP). It is a hereditary condition – thanks, mum. Although I was only four, I remember the day I was diagnosed vividly. It was Christmas Day; they tend to be memorable at that age. It had gone well, I received all the presents I wanted, and I got to spend time with my wider family. We spent most of the day at my gran's house, as we did every year. It was beginning to get dark, something that happens alarming early in the northeast of Scotland in the middle of winter. One of my cousins suggested going into the garden to play. Being extremely competitive, I had to be first. I raced out of the house and into the garden, pumping my arms as fast as I could. My cousins might be older and bigger than me, but I could beat them.

Just as I was about to celebrate my victory – bang! I ran straight into the pole that holds up the washing line. Inconsolable, shocked and confused, they took me back in to my mum. A big hug did much to put the world to rights.

My mum turned to my dad and asked, 'Do you think he's got it?'

'Yeah, I think he's got it.'

When you are four and you hear your parents discussing whether or not you have it, and you don't know what 'it' is, it's scary. Later that week, I was diagnosed with RP.

My condition is degenerative; I will almost certainly go blind at some stage in my life. When I was young my symptoms were less pronounced. I had slightly less peripheral vision than most people and my central vision was a bit blurry, but I managed fine. The only issue was when the light level was low. As a result, RP didn't affect me greatly in my early years, in fact, I doubt many people were aware of it. Over time, it became more of an issue and I would often find my limitations frustrating. It has always irked me when someone suggests I can't do something because of my disability.

I was a rather exuberant child. My parents let me try a number of sports, presumably to get me out of their hair and burn off some of my boundless energy. I tried everything: swimming, gymnastics, trampolining and even fencing. The thought of a visually impaired boy wielding a sword still makes me laugh. I discovered athletics at the age of ten and was immediately smitten. I'd found an outlet for my competitive nature. The simplicity and freedom of running as fast as you can was pure joy. It made sense to me. As my eyesight began to deteriorate, there was no issue as long as I ran in bright daylight or under floodlights. It provided a much-needed release for some of the frustrations that built up during my school day.

For years my education and sport went hand in hand. I was never a believer in cutting back on training during exams, quite the opposite. I felt that sport gave me the break I needed to switch off mentally and allowed me to go back to studying in a better frame of mind. Despite some issues with my eyesight, I did well in school. Crucially, though, I never truly found anything that inspired me as much as sport – first athletics and then cycling.

Reflecting on all these factors, I began to realise what my passion was and who I was as a person. I understand that pursuing your passion as a career isn't always an option, sometimes you have to do something else to enable your passion. But here I was in 2008 with the opportunity to compete at a home Paralympics in four years' time. I had a dream and I knew what made me tick: competition, overcoming challenges and proving the doubters who said I couldn't do it that they were wrong. This is what put fire in my belly and would get me up in the morning to push myself. The dream of competing at the Paralympics was the spark I needed; knowing who I was and what I needed out of life helped ignite it.

So how do you find what drives you? Some people just seem to know what their calling is. You are lucky if you're one of them; I've never found it that easy. There have been several times during my life where I have had to seriously consider what direction I want to take things. Taking the time to reflect and question myself has been vital. Having a favourite thinking place pays dividends; for me it's either walking the dog or in the shower. By taking the time to reflect, you realise just how far you have come and what you have to offer the world. Combine this with something that motivates you and you have the power to drive through any obstacles.

TAKE ACTION

We're all guilty of going about our daily lives, doing the things we need to do, rather than taking time for self-reflection. Find a place where you can do some serious thinking and ask yourself these questions.

- Why do I currently do what I do?
- What drove me to go down this route?
- What are the parts of my job that really interest me?

- What am I passionate about?
- What gets me fired up?
- When do I go on a rant or get really involved in a debate?
- What was the topic of discussion?

Genetics and background always play a part. Growing up, I always wanted to be a Formula One driver, unfortunately there's not much call for visually impaired drivers. This isn't me saying not to dream, but during the reflection time, you might have to rule out a couple of options. If you're in your early thirties and haven't kicked a ball in fifteen years, you're probably not going to make it as a Premier League footballer. Ask yourself:

- What am I good at?
- What skills have I picked up along the way?
- What things do I find challenging?
- What areas could I improve in?

Bear in mind, reflection isn't just a one-off thing. I've had to re-evaluate several times during my career and, on occasion, realise that my drive has changed. As you grow and develop this often happens – you may find yourself pivoting to something new. Don't be alarmed, it happens. Some people find it helpful to reflect at the end of each year, taking stock of where they are and where they want to be. Self-reflection is crucial to success. After all, how can you know where you are headed, if you don't know where you currently are and how you got there?

Invite opportunities

If you've worked through the Disrupt and Reflect steps, you are getting more understanding of the person you are and what makes you tick. Knowing what gets you fired up is a great starting point, but it's completely wasted if you don't do anything with it. In this section we look at how you can make the most of your newfound motivation in phase three of DRIVE: Invite opportunities into your life.

When working with my clients, I often ask what makes successful people champions at what they do. Take a moment to think about this. Think of successful people in different fields, someone from sport, someone from your line of work. What would you say are the key factors that helped them along the way? No doubt they have some natural talent for what they do. Other factors probably include a strong work ethic, a desire to succeed, good people skills and resilience. Are there any other factors? I'm sure you can probably think of a few people who have all these skills, but never amounted to much. One answer that always pops up in my seminars and workshops is luck. Almost everyone accepts that luck plays a part in success.

I would be lying if I claimed that luck hadn't played a part in my sporting career. Of course it has. I told you earlier about my chance encounter with Craig Maclean from British Cycling at Manchester velodrome. That meeting helped shape my cycling career. But was it luck that brought us together that day? I don't completely agree with the phrase, 'You make your own luck'. But I can say with confidence that you can certainly swing things in your favour. Had I not made a conscious effort to go to the National Cycling Centre for a taster session, I would probably have never met Craig. By making that decision and putting myself in the right place, I was *inviting opportunity*.

During my late teens and early twenties, I used to play poker. 'Texas Hold 'em' was my game of choice. Each player is dealt two cards face down, these are known as pocket cards. Five cards are then dealt face up in the centre of the table, known as community cards, which are used by all players. Your hand is made up with the best five cards of the seven available to you, two pocket cards and five community cards. Betting takes place long before you have all five cards, so much of your time is spent anticipating what might be dealt and what your opponents may have. The beauty of this game is that by looking at what cards are available to everyone, you can anticipate what your opponents may have.

In 'Texas Hold 'em', luck plays a big part; however, a few players are always more successful. Are they just inherently lucky people? I believe there is far more to it. In poker, you can swing the odds in your favour. This is done by reading your own situation and that of your opponents, as well as understanding the odds of specific cards being dealt. If you play with discipline, putting yourself in good situations rather than bad ones, you are far more likely to win.

So how does this play out in your career? I believe that the most successful people are indeed lucky, but they have also managed to swing the odds in their favour. There are two straightforward ways of doing this, putting yourself in the right place – as I did at the velodrome – and meeting the right people. Being visible is crucial to success. If people don't know who you are and what you are trying to achieve, they won't come along and offer you a leg up. If nobody knows you are branching out in a new direction, then opportunities won't come your way. There is already far too much noise out there; if your plan involves keeping your head down, you'll never stand out from the crowd. The first step is by dropping things into your daily conversations. By doing this you are planting a seed. You'd be surprised how many useful connections can be made through the network you already have.

Try it next time you get a phone call or meet up with someone. When they ask the inevitable, 'Hey, how are you?', rather than your usual one-word answer, try a new approach. Maybe tell them what you're aiming to do. For me it could be something like, 'Hey Neil, how are you?', 'Yeah good thanks. I'm writing a book at the moment and I'm trying to work out how to go about publishing it.'

At this stage, if my friend has no interest, they will move the conversation on. However, perhaps they know someone who has written a book before or know someone in the publishing industry. If they do, no doubt they will offer to connect me with that person. It's a simple adjustment to the way you communicate. Try it and see what opportunities come your way. We will be looking at the specifics of achieving your goals in the next section; this may give you a clearer picture of what you currently need help with.

The next stage is to put yourself in rooms with people who can help you progress. This could be a specific person. If, for instance, you hope to get a promotion at work, then you need to be visible to the people who make those decisions. Hard work will get you so far, but why not swing the odds in your favour? If you are in a room with one of your seniors, strike up a conversation. Take the opportunity to ask what they are working on and if there is anything you can do to help.

Asking people about themselves is the quickest way to strike up a relationship. If you can help them with an issue they might have, they are likely to look favourably on you in the future. Be aware if you are offering to help, you are not asking for anything in return. This is simply an exercise to expand your network and become more visible. By providing value to them, you will have gained their trust. This in itself has the potential to be extremely rewarding.

Networking events and conferences are fantastic opportunities to meet like-minded people. If you live in or near a major city, you will have no problem finding suitable events. You might view these as a waste of time, but in all likelihood, you will meet someone who can at least point you in the right direction. A useful trick can be to ask a question during any Q&A sessions. If worded correctly, a question can alert everyone in the room to the help you're seeking. Failing that, by talking to as many people as you can, you have the ideal opportunity to practise that conversational trick of telling people what you are up to and where you could use some help.

My final tip is to use social media to your advantage. The world has never been so well connected; why not get it to work in your favour? You can become better known in your industry by spreading your message to a wider audience. I've also found that it allows you to contact people who in the past would have been unreachable. This has worked extremely well for me. When I began performance coaching in 2017, there were certain elements of running a business that baffled me. I started to follow some big hitters from the business world on Twitter. I learnt a lot simply from the things they were tweeting about. Occasionally I would reply to, or share their tweets, and something incredible happened.

Phil Jones MBE, Managing Director at Brother UK, replied. I chose to follow Phil for several reasons. He is an immensely successful man who has been involved in business for many years. His tweets clearly show he has an interest in personal development. I also found out that Phil was a keen cycling fan. This meant I had an ace or two up my sleeve. We began chatting and decided to meet for a coffee in Manchester. It was the perfect opportunity to ask Phil a few questions about business and entrepreneurship. Being the generous man he is, Phil was only too happy to pass on nuggets he'd acquired over the years. The advice he gave me was incredibly useful and we continue to chat to this day. I was also delighted to deliver a keynote speech at their 2018 sales and marketing conference and meet other colleagues.

I also decided to follow one of Britain's leading business advisors, Daniel Priestley. I first learnt about Daniel from reading his book *Entrepreneur Revolution*.[2] I was instantly captivated. Everything he said made me realise that not only did I have the potential to create my own business, but to excel at it. I even encouraged my wife Lora to read it and ordered his other books.

Pre-internet this would have been the sum of our relationship. However, a simple tweet about how much I had enjoyed his book led Dan to message me back. After exchanging a few messages, Dan offered to have a chat on the phone with me. I'll be honest, I've never been so nervous to answer a call. I held Dan up on a

---

2   Daniel Priestley, *Entrepreneur Revolution* (Capstone, 2018)

pedestal as a great author and businessman. To my surprise, he was in awe of my achievements as a sportsman. Dan has an incredible way with words and is the master of metaphor. He passed on some incredible advice and explained it in a way that was simple to understand. Somewhat out of the blue, Dan offered me a place on his 'Key Person of Influence' course. It was an incredibly generous offer that was an absolute game changer for my business and is the reason you are reading this book. I still owe you, Dan.

TAKE ACTION

It's time to become visible and start inviting opportunities into your life. Here are a few angles of attack:

- Start dropping into conversation what you are working on and what you need help with
- Expand your network by talking to and connecting with others
- Attend networking events and conferences with an open mind
- Speak up during Q&A sessions
- Use social media to strike up conversations
- Spread your message online

In order to be a success, you need luck. By inviting opportunities to come your way, you swing the odds in your favour.

Vision

From speaking to clients and fellow athletes, I've come to the conclusion that as a person's career progresses, one of the key drivers is leaving a legacy. A vision for the future – phase four of DRIVE. Whether it's simply creating great opportunities for your family or changing the world for the better, there's something incredibly fulfilling about creating a legacy. Regardless of whether you are at the beginning or end of your career, a vision for the future can be a motivational multiplier. Anyone who has ever participated in team sport can testify that when you are no longer doing it just for yourself, your hunger to succeed substantially increases. Letting down those you care about hurts much more than just letting yourself down. Before you consider your vision for the future, it's important to understand why the desire to leave a legacy is so powerful.

When it comes to motivating both yourself and others, it's clear how to go about it, right? The carrot-and-stick approach has been the favourite method. If you want to get more out of someone, reward them. What could be a better performance incentive than a cash bonus at the end of the year? Similarly, if someone isn't performing, punish them, whether it be with a verbal warning, no bonus or grounding (in the case of a child). It's simple, straightforward and effective.

To prove the effectiveness of this model, several experiments have been carried out over the years. One such experiment took place in the USA in 1973. Psychologists Mark R Lepper and David Greene wanted to see what impact rewards would have on children aged three to five.[3] Fifty-one children were randomly split into three groups. Each child was invited into a room and given the opportunity to draw for six minutes. The first group was told that they would receive a certificate with their name on, complete with gold seal and ribbon if they decided to draw. Group two were not told about the reward and were given it as a surprise at the end of the six minutes if they had drawn. Group three were not told about and did not receive a reward, regardless of whether they drew or not.

Over the following weeks, the children's enthusiasm for drawing was observed in a classroom environment. The findings were startling. Lepper and Greene discovered that those who were in group one showed dramatically less interest in drawing in the later sessions, whereas groups two and three showed similar levels. Those who had been told they would be rewarded (offered a carrot), ended up enjoying the task less in the long run.

What this and many other similar experiments show, is that rewarding can be dangerous. What tends to happen is that an extrinsic motivator, like money or

3   M R, Lepper, D, Greene & R E Nisbett, 'Undermining children's intrinsic interest with extrinsic reward: A test of the "overjustification" hypothesis', *Journal of Personality and Social Psychology*, (1973), 28(1), pp129–137, https://doi.org/10.1037 /h0035519

a nice shiny certificate, may help performance in the short-term. However, performance will deteriorate significantly over time. The reason for this is that it undermines our intrinsic motivation – the motivation you feel within yourself to complete a task. Intrinsic motivation is what drives you to want to better yourself and to seek out new challenges. It is often driven by enjoyment or an interest in the task itself, rather than for any rewards for completing the task.

So we have to question whether the carrot-and-stick model really works to get top performance. This is not to suggest that seeking rewards, such as higher pay, is a bad thing. In fact, wanting to provide for the future and your family is important. The issue of reduced motivation occurs if you are doing something purely for the financial reward. Look at what tends to happen over time. The task becomes more and more of a chore and enthusiasm drains away. Think what happens if you offer a child a financial reward to do the dishes. Initially they are highly motivated, the lure of cash is strong. But within weeks or even days, the reward no longer seems worth it. In this situation you're left trying to bribe them with bigger rewards and the cycle continues.

Look back at the steps you have taken so far, particularly regarding your dream. Is your dream an intrinsic or extrinsic motivator? We want to ensure that you can give your all on a day-to-day basis over a long period of time. If your target is purely extrinsic, you may find your enthusiasm wanes before too long.

I became aware of the intrinsic versus extrinsic motivation debate during my time on the British Athletics team. Up to that point athletics had been a hobby. I dedicated a great deal of time to it because I enjoyed it and wanted to better myself. I started competing at the age of ten and initially was very successful, breaking the club sixty-metre record and winning the club championship one-hundred metre title for my age group. At the age of thirteen, something terrible happened – puberty. Actually, in my case, it didn't happen (at least not then). All the other boys got bigger and stronger and I didn't.

I was playing catch up for the next four years and during that time my sporting career suffered. I finished last in almost every race. Despite this, I enjoyed challenging myself and trying to break my own personal bests. I loved training and pushing myself harder than I ever had before. Eventually, I started to see results; by the age of seventeen I started beating a few people again.

Something changed when I signed up to British Athletics in my early twenties. Initially I loved it, I was getting paid, albeit a small amount, to do what I loved. But as I got into the hard training during the cold winter months, something I'd previously relished, I found my motivation had slipped. It started to feel like a job. Having gone from someone who did this as a hobby, to someone who had access to support staff and financial reward, my performance should have excelled. Instead it plateaued.

During late 2007 and early 2008 I started to resent the sport I once loved. I pushed myself as hard as I could, but that crucial extra 1 to 2% was missing. It wasn't until my forced exit from athletics, and my subsequent sport change, that I experienced that inner desire to succeed at something; the opportunity to learn a new skill and see how far I could push myself. It was then that I also started to consider what I would like to be remembered for. Some may consider this a slightly morbid pursuit, but I think it's quite the opposite. When it comes to intrinsic motivation, this is a recurring theme. It is one that many don't start to feel until they are well into their career. Crucially though, it's something almost everyone experiences – a desire to leave a legacy.

Having a vision for your future and beyond is an exceptionally intrinsic motivator. I'm sure you'd love to be remembered for something, even if it's just by those you hold dearest to you. How must it feel to have people look back fondly on what you have achieved in your life? If you have a vision, you can make that happen.

Looking back at my career, specifically at what has driven me, I realise that I always had an underlying vision. A desire to prove to the world that people with a disability can compete and excel at the same tasks as able-bodied individuals. When I was young this would often manifest itself as a chip-on-the-shoulder 'prove them wrong' approach. Over recent years it has transformed into a desire to showcase the incredible level of performance that para-athletes can achieve.

My goal has always been to go faster and be stronger than my able-bodied counterparts. If I can elevate the level of performance in my sport to achieve this, then I have done my job. My desire is to show others that they are capable of achieving great things, regardless of their perceived shortcomings. This is what drives me every day.

TAKE ACTION

Creating a legacy doesn't happen overnight, it takes time. If you have a vision for the future, you can start to shape it. Wanting to do it for someone else, not just yourself, gives an added level of accountability and, ultimately, drive.

Take this opportunity to think again about what drives you, look back at your reflections. Ask yourself:

- Why do I behave the way I do?
- What do I want to be remembered for?
- What impact do I want to have on the world?
- What will be my legacy?

Those with a vision for the future are often described as driven. Find your vision and you too can find your drive.

Remember, drive is the first step on the journey to Earn Your Stripes.

Energy

Without a shadow of a doubt, one of the main stumbling blocks on the journey to the top is inaction. If you've ever delayed too long over a decision or looked back with regret at not giving something a go, you are certainly not alone. If you are going to Earn Your Stripes, this is something that has to change. Motivation counts for nothing without the Energy (phase five of DRIVE) to act.

This sounds straightforward enough, but reality is a little different. For a start, most opportunities are far from clear cut. Often decisions involve some kind of compromise. By choosing to do this, I can no longer do that. I could do this, but I can't be certain of the outcomes. This brings in an element of doubt, something which your brain doesn't particularly like.

Thankfully, the human brain is programmed to protect you from danger. You don't want to be dawdling across the road with a bus hurtling towards you. In this situation, your brain alerts you to the potential danger, and you instinctively know to get moving. Unfortunately, your brain can be overprotective, keeping you safe from any perceived dangers. The part of your brain – often referred to as the lizard brain – controlling self-protection, works from a perfectly logical standpoint. It determines that you are currently safe as you are, all systems are working fine and there is no apparent threat. It believes that anything 'new' has the potential to remove you from this safe state. Your lizard brain perceives change as a new experience and therefore something to be avoided. This can be extremely limiting. No doubt without change you will live to see another day, but how can you ever expect to improve, to move forward or to experience new and exciting things?

There is a common name for this state. It is known as the 'comfort zone'. It's a place where you have become satisfied with your daily routine, happy to continue with the status quo. On the whole, it sounds like a good thing. As the name implies, who doesn't want to be comfortable? Remaining in your comfort zone, you don't have to deal with those uncomfortable, nerve-wracking situations where you have to step into the unknown.

I'm sure you've been in a situation where you've been nervous. Perhaps before a presentation, an interview or even the birth of your child. Try to remember the feelings you were experiencing. On edge, breathing a little faster than normal, an uncomfortable feeling in your stomach. It's quite common to lose your appetite when you are nervous. This is how I have felt on many a race day.

What's actually going on in our body when we feel like this? First let's look at the fear response. Imagine you're walking home late at night, as you round a corner someone is standing in front of you, you spot a glint of something shiny in their hand. In order to ensure survival, your brain is tuned to react quickly and efficiently. Information is quickly sent to the amygdala, a small almond-shaped part of the brain. The amygdala then sends a signal to the autonomic nervous system. Your body is now readying itself for the classic fight-or-flight response. Adrenaline and cortisol are released, which in turn cause several other hormones to be released. As a result, your heart rate quickens, increasing the blood flow to your muscles. Your breathing becomes more rapid, allowing more oxygen to reach the muscles needed in this situation. Your pupils dilate and muscles tense. Even the tiny muscles attached to each hair on your skin tense, forcing the hairs to stand on end. I'm sure this is a sensation you are familiar with. Finally, non-essential systems, such as digestion, are shut down; your focus is directed totally on the threat.

In a matter of seconds, you are primed and ready to either fight your potential attacker or turn and flee. Of course, this is an extreme example and the response is perfect to survive the ordeal. Frustratingly though, our minds struggle to distinguish between something life-threatening and something just a bit out of the ordinary. For instance, when you are going for that job interview. Your body responds in much the same way: the feeling of restlessness, elevated heart rate and sick feeling in your stomach. Rather than trying to remain calm by subduing these feelings and pretending that everything is fine, you can use the fear response to your advantage.

The fear response acts remarkably like that of excitement. The same hormones are released, and you may experience the same symptoms. But you interpret them in a completely different way. If you are going to see your favourite band, you are probably filled with excitement. This will cause you to be restless and alert. Your heart rate will speed up and you may even have butterflies in your stomach. Sound familiar?

This is precisely the same response to the fear response. It's very clear to see the crossovers when you think about what gives some people thrills. A rollercoaster can either be a thrilling or terrifying experience. The same could be said about skydiving or watching horror movies. Your response is determined by how you react to the situation. You tend to shy away from something that causes you anxiety but lean towards something that causes excitement.

On a race day I still get very nervous. Some people find the idea of racing in a high-pressure event an absolute no-go. I like to turn it to my advantage. It's no surprise that world records are broken at major events. It is when the pressure is extreme, the adrenaline release biggest and associated response at its most acute. If you channel it the right way, you are capable of performances far greater than you might achieve on any other day.

Why would we want to leave the safety of the comfort zone? Well, nothing much fun ever happens there. If you want to experience new things and continue to grow as a person, then you have no choice but to step out and face the big, scary world. But wait, we know it's not scary. It's actually the big, exciting world. Perspective is everything.

Having enough energy to take action can be daunting. Sometimes it means making some fairly bold decisions, but the pay-off can be huge. I had to make such a decision in 2009. Following my decision to give cycling a try, I decided to commit full-time to it. This was very much against the advice of many friends and coaches from the athletics community. They believed I should stick with athletics and see what happens. I think some thought I was rather naive and big-headed to assume I had enough potential to make it in another sport.

Despite understandable doubts, I was very driven. I ploughed ahead and after a trial day with British Cycling, I impressed them enough to be offered a place on their development squad. I was living at home at the time with my parents in Aberdeen. They were incredibly encouraging and happy to support me. Living rent free was a godsend as I only had a small pot of savings and no source of income, other than the £1,000 British Cycling were offering for the year.

The British Cycling Team is based at the National Cycling Centre in Manchester. It's a centralised system; riders who are on the programme are expected to live and train in the area, so that they can access all of the facilities and support staff housed within the velodrome. As a development rider, there was no obligation for me to live in the area, but I recognised that if I was to improve and make the most of this opportunity, then I needed to be there.

I decided to take the plunge and rent a flat in Manchester with one of the other guys on the squad. My few thousand pounds wouldn't go very far. It was do or die, or at least do or move back in with mum and dad. I love my parents dearly, but that wasn't an option. I had a matter of months to prove my worth to British Cycling. I moved to Manchester on 1 June 2009. I'd heard horror stories about Manchester (unfounded) and I was moving away from Aberdeen, and home, for the first time. It was a long way out of my comfort zone. But I knew that if I was going to succeed, this is what I had to do.

The first few weeks were both exhilarating and nerve-wracking. Learning how to fend for myself, while getting the most out of training full-time in a sport I was a novice at, was exhausting. I made rapid improvements and used the facilities and staff as much as I could. I had the opportunity to train with reigning Paralympic Champion pilot Barney Storey. Barney had won double gold with visually impaired rider Anthony

Kappes at the Beijing Games. Anthony had decided to take a year away from tandem racing. This meant he would not be competing for a place on the World Championship team that year. The championships were to take place in Manchester.

This was an absolute door-opener for me. I jumped at the opportunity and did everything I could to impress the coaches and Barney. After a summer getting to grips with cycling, getting physically in shape and learning how to fend for myself, we went into a selection process. The spot to ride with Barney at the World Champs was between myself and ex-judo Paralympic Champion Simon Jackson. Simon had switched sports the previous year so had a head start on me. He is an incredible character, one of the most likeable people you will meet. He was loved by everyone in the team, including myself. When it came to the selection process though, he was the enemy. It was him or me.

We went through a gruelling four weeks of training. Throughout every training session we were closely scrutinised. Knowing how important this was to my career – get this spot or go home – I ensured I was firing on all cylinders. I started strongly and Simon was on the back foot. We were both aware of our performance and the psychological advantage of getting ahead early paid off. I won the trial and was given the opportunity to ride with Barney.

On Friday 6 November 2009, I competed in my first cycling World Championships. I had lost my funding from British Athletics in late September 2008, so this was a remarkable turn of fortune. I can assure you; I was extremely nervous; this was all so new to me. I couldn't just slip into default mode as I would when racing in athletics: I didn't really have a default mode yet. I planned out my day with the help of Barney and my coach Chris Furber. I needed a blow-by-blow account of what I had to do and when. Today was the one-kilometre time trial. Four laps of the 250-metre velodrome against the clock, one bike on the track at a time, fastest time wins.

My stomach had been churning all day. I had to force myself to eat at the right times because my appetite had gone. I was restless and struggling to occupy my mind. All the classic fear response traits. As I made my way to my bike at the race start, I could feel my hairs standing on end, my heart beating fast and my breath quickening. 'This is what you came here for, Neil. This is what you wanted. This is what you live for.' My parents were in the stand watching, I didn't want to go home with them. It wasn't a huge crowd but there were certainly a few hundred people cheering us on. 'You can do this. Focus on what you've done in training, let's show everyone what you are capable of.'

The race began. During the kilo, you don't notice what's going on in the stadium. As we crossed the line on the first lap, though, I was aware of an announcement, followed by a roar from the crowd. My adrenaline levels must have been through the roof. With each passing lap I'd hear another garbled announcement followed by a roar.

We came round to complete the fourth and final lap. The kilo is an exhausting event. It's the perfect distance to cause an extreme rush of lactic acid that hits you like a wall at the finish. It's practically debilitating. As I gulped in the oxygen, I heard one last roar. As we rolled under the giant scoreboard, I looked up and saw, 'New world record'.

Despite having to be helped off the bike because my legs wouldn't function, I was elated. I was a world champion and a world record holder. That night I slept with my world champion jersey and gold medal on my bedside table. Every so often, I would wake up and reach out to check they were still there and smile to myself. To top it off, we returned two days later to win a second gold in the sprint event, again breaking the world record. My dream had turned into a fairy tale. In the space of one year, I had gone from losing my funding, being unemployed, going through some of the darkest days of my life, to being a double world champion and double world record holder. This was beyond my wildest dreams. I spoke to my parents afterwards and informed them that I wouldn't be going home with them.

TAKE ACTION

You can only start to drive when you add energy. The action you need to take at this stage is to use the energy created from your motivation to take action. Get out there and get noticed.

By picking up this book and reading it, you have already taken a step towards taking some form of action. During this chapter we have looked at finding your drive, the first of five stripes in the Earn Your Stripes methodology. This is what we've covered so far:

Disrupt – Things will only change if you disrupt your normal routine and way of thinking. Break free from the mould, think about your big dream and visualise it.

Reflect – Look back over your life and find out what make you tick. Look for patterns in behaviour over the years, think about what gets you excited and what you could live without.

Invite opportunities – Turn the odds in your favour by expanding your network and growing your knowledge. To be in the right place at the right time, you need to be somewhere other than where you are now.

Vision – Consider your legacy; intrinsic motivators ensure maximal performance. How would you like to make a difference in the world?

Energy – Make bold decisions; be brave and step outside your comfort zone.

There is a world out there for the taking, you can only get it if you step outside.

Summary

You're ready to take on the world. In the next section we look at how you go about it. If we put your new-found DRIVE to good use, by creating a structured and calculated plan of action, there will be no stopping you. If that sounds like something you are interested in, then read on.

Stripe Two: Performance

Now that you've found your DRIVE, let's look at how you can use it. To be a high performer, it's essential to understand performance itself. In this section we look at how you can set seemingly unattainable goals and break them down into their constituent parts. We explore how you can make performance gains in an array of areas, moving you closer to your ultimate goal.

Performance plateau

Performance is something I've spent significant amounts of time and effort on during my sporting career. After a lot of experimentation and with the knowledge gleaned from my time with British Athletics, British Cycling and my work with clients, I'm confident I have the most effective system to increase performance. In sport, we constantly seek to make tiny improvements, a tenth of a second here, a tenth of a second there, that make the difference between a gold medal and not even making the team. The search for these improvements is relentless; no stone is left unturned.

Before we get into this, I'd like to share a serious frustration of mine. In both business and sport, there's an all too common occurrence; people failing to reach their full potential. I've seen it countless times and no doubt it will continue to happen. Generally, individuals reach a high level of performance, climbing the ladder, until one day they get stuck, unable to ascend the final few rungs to greatness. I like to call this the 'performance plateau'. This tends to play out as follows. You start something new – a job or a sport. You learn fast and your rate of progression is rapid. This causes a great deal of pleasure and so you work a bit harder. You still see rapid improvement and get both the intrinsic and extrinsic rewards that go with it: the feeling of progression, the congratulations of others, perhaps the added incentive of financial reward.

As you move up the ladder, the rate of progression starts to ease off. This is inevitable as it's a lot tougher to improve something you are already good at. It's why elite athletes have to strive to find that extra tenth of a second or two. As your rate of progression starts to slow, you commit to working harder and harder. The initial joy is long gone and the whole process begins to feel like a grind. The rate of progression inevitably slows down, until eventually it either becomes undetectable or completely stagnates. You are now at a performance plateau.

This is a tricky place to be as you are probably working incredibly hard. In your mind, the only way to improve is to work even harder, but there simply aren't enough hours in the day. People may be advising you to take a different approach, try something new. In reality, the last thing you want to do is stop doing what you are doing, for fear that your performance will slip even further, and you find yourself in a far worse place. So now you are stuck.

Where do you go from here? Some people will decide enough is enough; they choose to start a different journey, destined to repeat the same process in another field or industry. Who can blame them, though? Humans like to challenge themselves. The lure of another career path where you can make rapid progression can be extremely tempting.

For those who stick it out, they may eventually assume that they have reached their level. Although they have always dreamed of making it to the top, maybe it's just not meant to be for them. Slowly but surely, they slip into a daily routine, doing just what's needed. They may be able to maintain their performance for a while, but inevitably, as their enthusiasm decreases, so too will their performance. In a business sense, they are the ones who stick out the same job for years, despite unhappiness and often resentment. It pays the bills and ensures their family lives a good life. While this is very worthy – and some people have no other choice – it frustrates me to see people choosing an option that doesn't fulfil them.

There have been occasions in my career where I have been at a performance plateau. Most notably between 2006 and 2008 when my performance on the athletics track stagnated. What had happened? I began to lose my motivation and I continued doing what I had always done, for fear of letting my performance drop. In fact, I had entered a comfort zone. There were opportunities for me to move away from home, find a new coach and try something completely different. A lack of self-belief meant I was too concerned about any potential negative outcomes. 'Making changes might mean I get worse and I might not qualify for the Paralympic Games. Best just stick with what I know and try a bit harder.' What happened? Nothing, zero progress, nothing ventured, nothing gained.

TAKE ACTION

First, we need to begin with a little self-reflection. This is something you have to get used to. By nature, athletes become very adept at looking back at a training session or race, analysing every detail to see where they could have improved. We look into debriefing skills in the next chapter, but for now, ask yourself the following questions:

- Are you still making improvements?
- Do you feel as though you are stuck?
- Is there scope to climb the ladder or take your business to the next level?
- Are you a believer in 'If at first you don't succeed, work harder'?

If you are at a performance plateau, don't worry. The solution isn't to work harder. Usain Bolt doesn't need to run 100m in 9.5 seconds every day, he just needs to do it when it counts. He works hard, yes, but he also works smart. I challenge you to work smarter, let's learn how to go about it.

Marginal gains

Breaking through a performance plateau only comes by having a philosophy that you stick with. Simply working hard and putting in the hours doesn't cut it. One such philosophy, the 'aggregation of marginal gains', has been made famous by British Cycling over recent years. It is the belief that a small number of improvements, in a number of areas, will improve your performance overall, breaking you clear of the performance plateau.

Sir Dave Brailsford was appointed Performance Director at British Cycling in 2003. Along with a new level of professionalism, he brought a new ethos to the team. Since then, the results at both the Olympic and Paralympic Games speak for themselves.

	Gold	Silver	Bronze
Sydney 2000			
Olympics	1	1	2
Paralympics	0	2	0
2003 – Dave Brailsford appointed Performance Director			
Athens 2004			
Olympics	2	1	1
Paralympics	3	3	2
Beijing 2008			
Olympics	8	4	2
Paralympics	17	3	0
London 2012			
Olympics	8	2	2
Paralympics	8	9	5
Rio 2016			
Olympics	6	4	2
Paralympics	12	3	6

Despite Dave's departure from British Cycling following the London 2012 Games, success continues to flow. What is this magical system that has led the National

Cycling Centre in Manchester to be dubbed the 'medal factory'?

First, we need to look at the inspiration behind this concept. Kaizen, a Japanese philosophy meaning 'continuous improvement' was made famous in 1986 by Masaaki Imai, in his book *Kaizen: The Key to Japan's Competitive Success*.[4] In this he discusses 'doing little things better, setting and achieving ever higher standards'.

This philosophy was widely used to rebuild Japan after World War II. The Toyota Motor Corporation was perhaps the most notable follower of this philosophy. Kaizen is deeply embedded in Toyota's core values and practised on a daily basis by all employees, from the CEO to the production line. It has ensured a tremendous level of success for Toyota; in 2017 they were the second largest automotive company in the world and the fifth largest company by revenue.

Innovation has always played a huge role in Toyota's success, ensuring they are market leaders in both hybrid electric and hydrogen fuel-cell vehicles. The Prius range had sold over six million units as of January 2017. A blueprint for the principles and philosophies

---

4   Imai, Masaaki (1988), *Kaizen: The Key to Japan's Competitive Success* (McGraw-Hill, 1986)

used by Toyota was first published in *The Toyota Way 2001*.[5] This focuses on two key areas: continuous development and respect for people.

These concepts from *The Toyota Way* alongside the ideology of 'marginal gains' has been widely used as a managerial tool by many companies across the world in various industries. It is what inspired David Brailsford to develop the aggregation of marginal gains model at British Cycling.[6] By making small, or even minute improvements in different areas, you can make a big overall gain. The process starts with looking at events and riders in great detail. The events are broken down into their key components and analysed. The next step examines what it would take to be the best in the world in each of those components. British Cycling are only interested in medals. In performance-based sport, medals mean funding – only the best will do. Inevitably, the decisions to work with certain individuals and not others can be ruthless.

Let's look at one of my events: the tandem kilo. As I've mentioned, it's a race against the clock and four laps of the track. If we break the event into its key components, you can see a natural split into the four laps. But this

---

5   The Toyota Way 2001 (2012), www.toyota-global.com/company
     /history_of_toyota/75years/data/conditions/philosophy
     /toyotaway2001.html

6   Eben Harrell, 'How 1% Performance Improvements Led to Olympic
     Gold', *Harvard Business Review*, 2015) https://hbr.org/2015/10/how
     -1-performance-improvements-led-to-olympic-gold

is nowhere near specific enough, we need to delve much deeper. For instance, at the start of the race a countdown clock counts you in. The starting gate is triggered to release the bike the instant the clock hits zero. Electronic timing systems allow us to calculate the time between the gate releasing and the point that the bike starts moving. Essentially, it's the reaction time. The ideal scenario is to get it as close to zero as possible. Many riders may lose two to three tenths of a second here: this can be the difference between winning and losing. Despite the race taking about 60 seconds, saving a couple of tenths of a second before you even start pedalling is huge. This split second is just one of several key components in this event.

Once we identify all the components of the race, we look at what the best in the world are doing, whether we can match this, and how we go about doing it. Going back to the previous example, looking solely at reaction time, there are several ways to improve it. Although different clocks are used at different events, they are all calibrated so that a second lasts as long as it should, exactly one second. Therefore, you realise that it's not about reaction time at all – it's simply going at the exact time you know the starting gate releases you. Repetition, visualisation techniques, refining your rhythm are all ways of improving. By syncing your breath to the sound of the beeps in the last five seconds of the countdown, you can improve your rhythm, ensuring you burst out of the starting gate at the strike of zero.

Another factor in the start of the race is the ability to press on the pedals to generate instant forward momentum. This relies both on torque, the force applied to the pedals to make them turn, and technique, the ability to channel that force in the right direction (forwards on the track).

Now we're torquing! I'm sorry, torque-based puns are inevitable in my line of work. Breaking it down further, how can we improve torque? Again, there are many ways, but strength is a key contributor. Lifting heavy weights is highly beneficial. Training on larger gears also works well. From a technique point of view, continuous repetition is vital, as well as video and coach feedback. We analyse in minute detail what happens during a start, make improvements and repeat.

As you can see, to save two to three tenths of a second, we're already getting quite deep. Imagine what would happen if you could save that much time in every component of your race? The performance gain by the end could be enormous. This could be the difference between mediocrity and outright supremacy. At British Cycling we don't just stop there, there's plenty more can be done. It's not just doing the right things in training and on race day, there are many day-to-day factors that go into high performance.

High performance is a lifestyle choice. It's important to ask yourself the tough questions. For instance, would I have performed better in training today, had I not stayed up an extra hour to watch television? There are performance gains all around you and at British Cycling we consider the lifestyle of riders. If you can ensure an elite athlete is at their best every day, they will get far more out of every single training session. We look at all areas of life and experts are brought in to cover rider needs in areas such as psychology, physiology, health, nutrition and lifestyle. Lifestyle includes assistance and advice on how to deal with the daily stresses and rigours of life. This can range from dealing with landlords, finding mortgage advisors, to looking at educational needs.

The beds in the villages at the Olympics and Paralympics are notoriously uncomfortable. Everyone knows how performance can suffer after a bad night's sleep. In the lead up to London 2012, each rider was given a travel mattress. This went to the holding camp in Newport with us, as well as on to the village. This ensured each rider got a better night's sleep than they otherwise would. I usually take my own pillow all over the world when I go to races. The last thing I need is to wake up on race day with a sore neck.

The working environment is also crucial; changes were made around the velodrome to make it more efficient. The dust build-up in the mechanics room was found to have a negative impact on bike maintenance. As a result, the floor was painted white so that any dust or dirt in the room was spotted quickly and removed. British Cycling is also famous for pushing the boundaries of aerodynamics. They work with experts from Formula One, using the wind tunnel to test all types of equipment to discover what works best on the velodrome. Every area has to be explored.

TAKE ACTION

The idea behind this philosophy is that each individual improvement isn't daunting. Just look at one or two things you could do better. Ask yourself:

- Can my performance be broken down into key components?
- Do other areas of my life impact on my work performance?
- What one thing in my life could I do just a little bit better?

What may seem like an exhaustive process, doesn't need to be put in place overnight. By focusing on a few small goals at a time, you achieve success in each area that cumulatively has a positive impact on the journey towards the overall vision.

Environment

Making improvements in something you are already good at is a challenge. Rather than drilling down into how you can be better at what you do, why not chase a few small, easy wins to get you started? As an elite athlete, it goes without saying that you should be living a life that is conducive to top-level performance. You need to have a good diet, regular sleep schedule and healthy lifestyle to get through training. If you want to be elite at what you do, shouldn't you be doing the same?

The environment you create around you will have an immediate impact on your performance, regardless of your career choice. If you're the kind of person who puts in a big shift at work before heading out for some drinks and a burger, or if you work late into the night and get up at the crack of dawn, are you allowing yourself the opportunity to get the most out of yourself?

I consider diet, sleep, exercise, life choices and the working environment I create, all vital to my success over the years. In this section we look at how you can feel better about yourself, have more energy and find more pleasure in what you do. I know the thought of a healthy diet and regular sleep schedule sounds dull, I felt the same way, but I came to realise that it's actually enjoyable. You learn that if you do things well most of the time, you can still enjoy yourself as well. We are all human after all.

The biggest change for me was in 2009. Moving from Aberdeen to Manchester meant I had to fend for myself. It also meant I was in the British Cycling system and could learn from elite athletes who'd achieved incredible success. The first lesson I learnt was about creating a high-performance environment. The training sessions at the velodrome were very different to what I was used to. Riders would arrive well in advance with their bikes and equipment. We would sit in a circle and chat, but this was also the opportunity for riders and coaches to discuss the upcoming training session. Everyone was ready to go with clear aims and objectives. The moment the clock reached 2pm, we were on the track warming up. There was no messing around. As we rode around the track one after the other, we were a team. We might be doing different training sessions, but the group warm-up showed that we were in this together. Between our efforts, it was back to the circle to look at data and video analysis. Everything was focused on performance.

Images of the team's previous successes were all around the velodrome, reminders of what the riders were capable of. Motivational slogans adorned the walls of the corridors and the gym. Although it was a little in your face, there was no doubting that this team expected success. It was hard not to get caught up in the atmosphere. This was definitely an environment conducive to high performance. If you didn't give it your all, you'd struggle to fit in. I soon learnt that if I wasn't in the best shape possible for every training session, I'd fall behind.

Lora and I met through cycling in September 2009 and I'm delighted to say that we are now happily married.

Prior to meeting Lora, many of the choices I made were far from ideal. I particularly struggled with diet. I have always found it hard to grasp what I should be eating and when, fortunately this is an area that Lora excels in. I had decided in my childhood that I didn't like fruit or vegetables – like many Scots. My diet mainly consisted of meat, a sauce and either rice or pasta. The alternative was pizza. Other regular additions to my diet included cheese, chocolate and more chocolate. I was drastically lacking in any nutrients and struggled to get five a week, never mind five a day. Despite this diet, I was still performing at a decent level. The amount of training I did kept the weight off, but I did often struggle with fatigue, due to a lack of nutrients and sleep.

I was also struggling with my video gaming addiction. I still love gaming, but in recent years I made the tough decision to give it up. Once I start playing a game, I can become stuck in that world for hours. As an athlete, there are some benefits. It's key not to be too physically active between sessions. Sitting still and doing very little can be a challenge for some athletes, but not for those addicted to video games. I would regularly end up playing late into the night, often not going to bed until well after midnight. There was also the problem that my brain was generally very switched on after hours of edge-of-your-seat gaming action, and it would take me a while to fall asleep. You know you are addicted to gaming when you start dreaming about video games, something I did regularly.

Lora began to teach me the value of a good diet. Through her love of cooking and eating out, I began to fall in love with good food. I now have a varied diet and enjoy eating almost anything. Because I still train hard and because I am a firm believer in enjoying life, I am allowed to have the odd bit of cheese, chocolate and cake. Chocolate cheesecake anyone?

I started going to bed at 10pm and the routine improved my sleeping. All this began towards the end of 2009 and, of course, other factors played a part in my improvement. But if you compare my personal bests then to now, you can see between a 4 and 5% improvement in time alone. Who knows what the long-term health benefits might look like?

When you analyse your performance at a specific task, you often have a narrow focus. It is easy to forget the impact that your lifestyle choices will have in the days and weeks to come. This is why British Cycling's marginal gains approach was so important. It focused on all the factors that could impact on performance, ranging from things we did on the track, as well as off-track. What are the areas you could make small improvements in? Some changes will be easy to make; others, like my decision to finally give up video gaming, may not. Ask yourself how much you really want it and how much you are willing to sacrifice.

TAKE ACTION

Let's look at a few key areas where you may be able to make improvements.

Diet

A healthy diet can have a positive impact on both physical and mental performance. Have you ever felt tired, irritable or had trouble focusing on challenging tasks? This could almost certainly be solved with an improved diet. I wouldn't dream of going to a training session without any breakfast or after I'd had a burger and pint for lunch. Why should the high-performance world of business be any different?

Some simple rules I live by:

- Eat three meals a day, never skip
- Eat plenty of fruit and veg
- Ensure a balanced, colourful diet
- When possible eat natural food
- If you're hungry, eat
- Stay hydrated

For information on great tasting, healthy food, Lora has created a food blog.[7] It's full of great advice and a huge array of easy-to-make recipes.

Sleep

How much sleep do you get? Latest research suggests that we need a minimum of seven hours sleep a night:

---

7   Lora Fachie (2019), www.blindinglygoodfood.co.uk

somewhere between seven and nine is ideal. Anything less has dramatic effects on your performance both physically and mentally, as well as some serious health concerns. Sticking to a routine is best, if you can create a rhythm of sleeping and waking at a similar time every day, your body will adjust to this. Staying up late or getting up early to do extra work results in less work being done long-term.

Exercise

As an athlete this has never been a major concern for me, but I do know that after taking time off after the Paralympic Games, periods of inactivity affect me physically and mentally. The current NHS guidelines state that adults should be active daily,[8] with at least 150 minutes of aerobic activity every week – something like cycling or brisk walking. It's also advised that strength exercises that work all major muscles be undertaken on at least two days a week.

- What does your current exercise plan look like?
- Could you timetable more exercise into your week?

Environment

Being in an environment that gets the most out of you is desirable, but not always straightforward. Making changes in the workplace to make it more performance minded may not always be possible. You can make small changes, though. For instance, recent evidence suggests that taking a micro break of just forty seconds to look

---

8   NHS Guidelines, Exercise, www.nhs.uk/live-well/exercise

at greenery can reduce stress and improve subsequent focus and performance on a given task.[9]

An environment where you can take regular breaks of around ten minutes every fifty to ninety minutes also improves performance, focus and the ability to see the big picture.

- What does your work environment look like?
- Could you build breaks into your day?
- Could you work smarter, rather than longer or harder?
- What quotes and slogans inspire you?

Improving in all these areas will enhance your performance.

Strategy

Once you've ticked off some easy wins, it's time for the nitty-gritty. I've learnt over the years that improvement in sport doesn't simply come from repetition. Initially it might be the case, but after a while you are just repeating the same process and hoping to get a better outcome. Simply hopping on my bike and pedalling

---

9   Kate E Lee, Kathryn J H Williams, Leisa D Sargent, Nicholas S G Williams and Katherine A Johnson, '40-second green roof views sustain attention: The role of micro breaks in attention restoration', *Journal of Environmental Psychology* (June 2015), Volume 42, pp182–189, www.sciencedirect.com/science/article/abs/pii/S0272494415000328?via%3Dihub

as fast as I can every day doesn't mean I will improve at my specific event. Instead I have to break my event down into its core components, I need to analyse them and find ways to improve on the specific individual skills. Once I piece these together, then I will see improvement. This is the case in any industry and is something I often examine with clients. Improvement isn't merely a plan – do this and that will improve. Instead it's pulling together many aspects, all of which have a fluidity to them; in this section we are creating a strategy.

I am going to outline how I break my event down into its constituent parts, how I strategise for improvement, and the process involved in creating a constantly evolving strategy. Like business, the world of sport is constantly evolving. Planning what to do in four years' time to win the Paralympic Games doesn't always stack up by the time those four years have passed. Records have been smashed and the world has moved on. It is wise to hypothesise what might be needed but be aware that your strategy is not set in stone.

Where do we begin? Every four years I sit down with my team and talk about what time we think is needed to win the next Paralympics. For the 2020 Tokyo Games, we initially thought a time of 59.5 seconds would win, this has since been adjusted to 58.9 seconds. The next phase is to break this time down into the four laps that make up the kilo and work out how much each lap should take. This gives me an indication of where my strengths and weaknesses lie in comparison to these target times. The simple thing at this stage would be to ask, 'How can we improve each of these laps and hence improve overall?' With so many individual parameters affecting each lap, this isn't detailed enough.

We then break the race into its constituent parts. There is the moment that the bike is released from the starting gate, the first few turns of the pedals, the acceleration phase out of the saddle, the seated acceleration phase, the transition into a more aerodynamic position, hitting top speed, the line taken around the velodrome, the aerodynamic position itself, the tolerance to lactic acid build up, pedalling style under fatigue and so on. Then we have to consider the warm-up for the event, the mental side, nutrition and the equipment we compete on. There are many areas to consider and it's easy to become overwhelmed. The key thing to remember is that it is a four-year strategy, we don't expect to hit all these areas at once.

After breaking everything down into minute detail, we establish key areas where we think we currently fall short. These become our primary focuses. Picking one as an example, let's assume I was having issues accelerating the bike through the second quarter of the first lap. I like to call this the acceleration phase. If this was deemed to be a primary focus, somewhere we could gain valuable time, then we'd break this down further. The first question – what makes the perfect acceleration phase? In my opinion, perfection is rapidly increasing the speed of the tandem from under 50kph to over 60kph in the space of just over 60m. It involves both riders working in perfect synchronicity out of the saddle, applying maximum power to the pedals, with all power channelling the bike forwards. It involves using as big a gear as possible, as this will benefit later in the race, and it involves holding a steady line on the track, ensuring the shortest route is covered.

The next question is, 'How can I improve my acceleration phase if I'm aspiring for perfection?' Each of the above factors can be broken down further; I can work with specific members of staff to improve in each area and we can measure the overall improvements. For instance, acceleration is improved by increasing the power to weight ratio. I can aim to improve my power output, while also looking at how weight can be reduced. This could be personal weight, working with the nutritionist to ensure I am as lean as possible, or it could mean shedding weight from the bike itself, working with mechanics. My power output can be increased by specific power-based training on the bike, or by increasing my strength in the gym and converting this to power both in the gym and on the bike.

With regards to synchronicity and holding the correct line, this is best improved by training efforts on the tandem. The coach will give us feedback, while a performance analyst will film us so that we can look back to see what we've done well and what needs improvement. As with anything, in order to improve, repetition is required. We perform a training effort, discuss feedback with the coach, analyse times, watch footage, modify and repeat.

The final piece of the puzzle is to ensure that everything we do is measurable. Put simply, there is no way to know if you are improving if you can't measure your progress. The overall measurement is simple in this case, we time how long it takes us to complete the effort and see numerically if we are getting quicker. To do this we use a timing system linked to a transponder on our bikes. It means any timing errors are minimised. We calculate our speed at the end of each effort and see if we are improving – instant feedback.

Over the course of the four years, we work through different key areas of improvement, as well as timing peaks in our form with major races. It is an extremely challenging strategy to construct and takes significant orchestration, as well as experience. But get it right and the results can be mind-blowing.

Once the strategy is in place, it is vital to set smaller targets. During each training block, usually an eight-week period, I set five targets for myself. The aim is to complete all five in the allotted time. I usually achieve all five, but if I don't, I can either choose to carry them over to the next block or accept that I've made progress despite not hitting the target. I make sure each target or goal is in a different area. One is always gym-based. As a sprinter, I spend a lot of time in the gym and it is integral to my performance on the bike. The next three areas depend on the training block's focus. These could be endurance, acceleration, technique; essentially any of the areas we've broken things down into. My fifth and final goal is always something personal, something away from cycling. The reason for this is that in recent years I've found that a focus away from sport is hugely beneficial to my cycling performance. Because an off-bike focus is important, I always include one in my goal setting block. Below is a list of the five goals I undertook in summer 2019.

Area	Goal
Gym	Trap bar deadlift – a set of three reps at 235kg
Acceleration	Half lap from gate in 11.5 seconds on 115″ gear
Endurance	Increase three-minute average power on last block (346 watts)
Aerodynamics	Complete aero runs to establish optimal position
Personal	Complete first edit of book

I did manage to complete all my goals. Those of you who have heard of SMART goals will notice that these all comply. It's the belief that your goals should be specific, measurable, achievable, relevant and time-bound.

Specific: It's important to ensure the goal is something specific, for instance having a gym goal of 'getting stronger' doesn't really make things clear. If the goal is too open, the method by which you plan to improve isn't clear and so you are far less likely to succeed.

Measurable: It's vitally important to be able to measure progress. As a former gamer, I constantly strived to get enough experience to increase my level or earn enough points to unlock something new. Similarly, with lifting weights, if I see I am closing in on my target weight each week, it spurs me on. Gamify your goals.

Achievable: Setting goals that are unachievable is pointless, likewise with goals that are too easy. The sweet spot is finding a challenge that stretches you, but which you can complete with hard work.

Relevant: Having targets that relate to your end goal – mine being to stand on top of the podium in four years – is vital. Always have your end goal in mind when goal setting. You could argue my personal goal isn't relevant, but as I see my other life outside cycling as crucial to my success, it definitely ticks the box.

Time-bound: Finally, your goals must be time-bound. Most people function best when there is a deadline. Things without a deadline simply don't get done. All my goals are to be completed within my eight-week training block.

With your strategy in place and your goals lined up for short-term success, you are well on your way. The next step comes down to tracking your progress, debriefing and being adaptable. A strategy that never changes is merely a plan. Do not plan for your success, strategise.

TAKE ACTION

Consider your four-year goal. If you're struggling with this, look back at the Disrupt section in the previous chapter, where I asked you to dream big. What was the dream? I encourage you to write your four-year goal down. Evidence suggests that people who write their goals down are 50% more likely to succeed.

- Break your goal down into all its constituent parts, brainstorm all the possible things you need to achieve this. Think of someone who has already arrived at this goal and look at the skills or areas they excel at? Write your final list down and start to build a strategy. What are the areas where you could use improvement? Which tasks will take longer to implement and where are the quick wins?
- Think about how you can improve in these areas, what will take you from where you are now to the level you want to be? Look for measurables that will help you analyse your progress.
- Finally, set yourself a series of five goals in different areas over an eight-week period. This is long enough to get things done, but short enough not to let the goal get too far out of sight. Ensure your goals are SMART.

Take time to create your strategy and it will pay you back tenfold. This may well be the most important work that you ever do.

Progress tracking

Achieving targets makes us feel good, even small ones. Simply ticking something off on a to-do list can induce a spike in dopamine, bringing pleasure and satisfaction. This is why video games are so addictive, the lure of completing another challenge is just around the corner. You are constantly reminded of this with progress indicators, achievements and kill counts. We can learn from the video-gaming industry. It's possible to create progress indicators and achievements in your own life – probably not a kill counter, though.

When training at the athletics track during my teenage years, I found a method for getting through difficult sessions. Sport helped my maths, in particular fractions. As I struggled through my training efforts, I would work out the percentage or fraction completed so far, and therefore how much left to go. Ticking off another effort would mean a step forward on the progress bar. I might be suffering, but I'd know that the next effort would take me to four-to-go in my twenty-effort session, I would be four fifths of the way there. This is something I still do, particularly on endurance rides or sessions. By creating a progress bar in my head, I am winning the mental battle.

It's also possible to measure your progress against others. In a race environment, if I feel an opponent riding up alongside me, I always find something more.

I can dig in deeper than I otherwise would, finding that little bit extra to cross the line first. When you see where you are now, how far you've come and can visualise how far you still have to go, you strive to achieve. That dopamine rush is within sight and the sense of progress already achieved will give you the motivation to keep going. It's very rare that someone will quit something when they are more than halfway through, at that point you feel too heavily invested. A visual reminder will only strengthen your resolve.

Progress tracking is used throughout sport. On the whole, sport is very measurable, whether it be distance covered, time elapsed, points or goals scored. In cycling, we can look at timing splits through different phases of the race. We can analyse power outputs of riders through each of these phases. It's possible to review footage and analyse what is going on in super slow motion. We can track how many reps we do in training, what weights we lift in the gym and even measure our percentage of body fat. Elite sport is not always the life of glamour that you might imagine.

With technology developing on a daily basis, it's becoming far more straightforward to monitor data in a wide array of fields. You probably have a supercomputer in your pocket. Today's smart phone has over 1 million times the memory and 100,000 times the processing power than the computing power used by NASA to control the first lunar landing.[10] There are apps to track a range of things from your sleep quality and pattern to the number of sales your team is making. Whatever your targets are, it's essential to both your performance and strategy to find a way of tracking your progress to see where you lie on the journey.

Once your performance tracking measures are in place, it's time to create accountability. Nothing feels worse than letting other people down. Many people don't mind letting themselves down, but when other people are involved, it's a completely different mentality. This is where accountability comes in. If others are aware of your strategy, goals and targets, you are far more likely to endeavour to complete them. Equally the benefit of having others know what you are striving for makes it more likely you have their support.

I have accountability on several levels in my sport. First, I have a team to answer to. My team of experts at British Cycling know my goals and are part of them. They support me and strategise with me. Together we plan for success: I have no intention of letting them down. Next is the fact that my funding is awarded on an annual basis. The level of funding for the following year is dependent on my performance the previous season. This is the cut-throat world of sport. World

---

10   Graham Kendall, 'Would your mobile phone be powerful enough to get you to the moon?' *The Conversation* (2019), https://theconversation.com/would-your-mobile-phone-be-powerful-enough-to-get-you-to-the-moon-115933

Champion one year, if you fail to perform the next, you are off the squad without funding or support. As a result, there is another level of accountability regarding my race performances. It is how British Cycling and UK Sport judge me. While it brings an element of pressure, it also ensures maximum commitment.

My final accountability group are my training partners, my contemporaries. This is often the most powerful group. We are in it together. We push each other every single day, we suffer together and we succeed together. Continual development is much easier when there are others around you striving for the same thing. There are days when I love them and days when I despise them. When I'm at my lowest ebb, I know they will push me and I curse them for it, but it's what I need. Over the past few years, Pete Mitchell, Matt Rotherham, James Ball, Sophie Thornhill and Helen Scott have collectively suffered with me – thank you.

A key difference between a World Champion and your average athlete, is the willingness to show up every day. It is imperative for success that regardless of how you feel, you show up and do what you need to. There are days when I dread training, just as there are days when I love it. I need to show up on both occasions and I need to perform. A strong accountability group ensures this.

You may have heard of the race between two polar expeditions in 1912. The battle to be the first to reach the South Pole was between the British team led by explorer Robert Falcon Scott and the Norwegian team led by Roald Amundsen. It was a gruelling task and both expeditions took a serious amount of planning. The two expeditions had very different approaches to how they would reach the Pole. Scott's team planned to make use of good weather. They would trek as far as they could on good days and hunker down when the weather bit back.

In contrast, Amundsen's team decided to cover 15 to 20 miles every day, regardless of the weather. It was a challenging but achievable distance. It must have been difficult to have the discipline to stop even when the weather was favourable and, in contrast, have the drive to push forward on days when it was not. It was a team decision and they held themselves accountable to it. The simple act of showing up each day was crucial. Amundsen's team reached the South Pole before Scott's team. Furthermore, on the return journey, Scott's team struck disaster when they were hit by brutal weather conditions. They were forced to hunker down again in the tent. Supplies ran out and sadly the team perished. The moral of the story is to show up each day whatever the circumstances. Whether you feel like it or not, it's vital to your success. By showing up without fail you create a habit that becomes part of your normal routine.

TAKE ACTION

Look at your strategy.

- When considering your goals, find ways to track your progress.

- Use lessons from the video gaming world, create progress bars, give yourself rewards for successes, gamify everything. Monitor your progress in as many ways as you can and make sure it's accessible, perhaps using your phone so that you can easily review it; even something as simple as keeping a tally in your Notes app. Progress tracking is vital.

- Build levels of accountability into your strategy. A good start is by telling your partner your plans or posting a goal on social media. Ideally find a group of people who will hold you to your goals. You want a group who will question you if you aren't giving your all but will also be supportive during tough times. Are there any groups or networks you could join?

Find what works for you and be sure to turn up every single day.

Redefining failure

To succeed, you first need to fail – many times. I am not guaranteeing your success by following my methodology, in fact quite the opposite. I encourage you to fail, often and hard. The problem is that when we see the word 'fail' we associate it with negativity. In this section, I redefine what failure is and encourage you to seek it out.

As we grow up and become more aware of ourselves, we try to avoid failure at all costs. It is something that is generally frowned upon. In fact, we go out of our way to hide failures; embarrassed to let people see our mistakes. This is an exceptionally short-sighted attitude. It is only through failure that you learn from mistakes and make improvements. In his bestseller *Black Box Thinking: The Surprising Truth About Success,* Matthew Syed discusses the different approaches to failure in various industries. In particular, he looks at the difference between the aviation and healthcare industries.

The aviation industry is incredibly open when there is a fatal crash. Investigations begin immediately, all avenues are explored and recommendations for safety improvements are made. In contrast, the healthcare service, due to its culture and targets, has tended to cover up mistakes. It means that countless opportunities to learn can be lost which may lead to further incidents that could have been avoided.[11] Unfortunately, the aviation industry is in the minority, many industries are guilty of covering up, or placing blame on an

---

11   Sir Robert Francis, QC, *Freedom to speak up: An independent review into creating an open and honest reporting culture in the NHS* (2015), http://freedomtospeakup.org.uk/wp-content/uploads/2014/07/F2SU_web.pdf

individual. Fortunately, I am involved in an industry where failures and defeats come thick and fast, often in the public eye. You will have seen many sporting events where pundits analyse every move in super slow motion. It is possible to examine performance microsecond by microsecond. The failures are out in the open for all to see and most people tend to voice an opinion.

I can assure you that the same thing is going on behind the scenes. After each race, indeed after most training sessions, there is some form of debrief. If mistakes are made, we want to know why. Was it simply human error? What could we do differently next time? Most athletes do this automatically after a race, match or competition, whether they have won or not. How many athletes have you heard after achieving a personal best saying what they could have done better? I'm guilty of it, too. I've heard it being described as 'being too hard on yourself'; in reality it is the endless struggle for perfection. The constant search for areas to improve on, even when everything is going well, is what separates the average from the elite. Even after breaking world records, I look back on a race to identify where I could have improved. Why wouldn't I? In an ever-improving world, today's world record won't necessarily be good enough for me to medal next time.

In a world played out on social media, the assumption is that everyone is watching you. I believe this discourages people from attempting new things; they are scared of making a mistake and being judged. The reality is that people are too busy worrying about themselves to bother about you. I would encourage you to make mistakes – it is the only way you will improve. People say that in sport you lose a lot more than you win. This is especially true if you add up all the times you've failed to lift a weight in the gym, failed to hit a training target on the bike or failed to complete a tough training session. My failures really do add up. If you live your life close to your limit, failures are inevitable. It's only through failure that I can see where my limits lie. Then I can revisit my strategy and readjust as necessary. Without failure the strategy never adapts, and progress will be limited. This means your performance remains below your true capabilities.

Failures can hit hard, and I don't suggest they are always easy to take. Now and again you will fail big, and although plenty of lessons will be learnt, it may take a while to come to terms with it. Unfortunately, that's life. But deal with it the right way and that's when the biggest changes can happen.

It was 2016. Despite all the people, the Athletes' Village in Rio de Janeiro felt a lonely place. It was race day and, as usual, the nerves had kicked in. The previous four-year cycle felt like a dream – Pete Mitchell and I had gone undefeated in international competition. Along the way, I had added six more world championship titles to my haul, as well as breaking both my world records. Perhaps the greatest achievements had been finally breaking the 60-seconds for the kilo and the 10-seconds for the flying 200m. Life had been pretty good. Pete and I had just one race left to complete the four-year journey – the big one.

Pete joined the squad following on from London 2012. He had been an academy rider on the Olympic programme. This is for young athletes who are on the road to the top, but sadly Pete hadn't made that final step. Fortunately for me, he decided to switch to tandem piloting. Training and racing with Pete over the four-year cycle had been a real pleasure. He is one of those people who just loves cycling. He's a very calm and easy-going man, always keen to avoid conflict if possible. In all our time together, we barely had a disagreement; only when his laid-back attitude irked a stressed and serious me.

As we weren't racing until later in the day, we had some time to kill. Channel 4 was streamed live into the village so we could watch how our teammates were getting on, both in cycling and in other sports. We had spent hours in front of the TV over the previous couple of days. We were experts at killing time. As we watched the day's action, my face appeared on the screen. It was an interview we'd done a few months earlier.

'I've won every race I've done; we've gone pretty much the full cycle undefeated, it's just the big one to go now. If we do our best, it's going to take a hell of a lot to beat us.'

When it comes to accountability, there's nothing like telling the whole nation your intention. It suddenly felt a lot more real. Despite the nerves, there was an underlying feeling of confidence. Training had been going extremely well and I knew that we would go fast if we did everything right. We arrived at the velodrome in plenty of time and took the opportunity to soak up the magical atmosphere of the Games. The venue was full – of sound, of atmosphere. There are certain days where I understand the term 'an electric atmosphere', this was one of them. The hairs on my arms stood to attention, this was excitement, this is why I do what I do.

The one-kilometre time trial is seeded, meaning that as defending Paralympic Champions, reigning World Champions, and therefore favourites, we were last to go. As I warmed up on the static bike in the track centre, I watched my rivals' races, nothing blisteringly quick. I knew we could beat them. The bike before us was the pair from the Netherlands. On the back was the young debutant Tristan Bangma, just 19 years old and already a medallist at the World Championships. In contrast, his pilot Teun Mulder was highly experienced and a legend in track cycling. He was a bronze medallist in the keirin at the London Olympics where Chris Hoy had won gold. Teun had achieved at the highest level. A three-time World Champion during his solo career, Teun had switched to tandem piloting. Although Pete and I had gone undefeated over the previous four years, the Dutch boys were always pushing us. They were why we were as good as we were. I knew they would put in a strong performance; I knew they would be hard on our heels.

The Dutch team were fast: they broke the magical 60-second barrier to become the first bike to ever do this at sea level (our world record was at altitude in Mexico). 59.822 seconds was seriously fast. I knew we could beat it, we'd also planned to break that barrier at these Games. As the dramatic pre-race music blared, we walked towards our bike in the starting gate. Towards our destiny. I took a deep breath and did my best to project confidence and determination. I got onto the bike behind Pete: I was ready.

The countdown clock started ticking down, 'This is it, four years' work, one chance'. As the clock hit zero, we burst out of the starting gate. Our acceleration out of the saddle around the bend and into the back straight felt strong and rapid. We sat down and continued to drive the bike forwards through the banking and across the line to complete the first of four laps. Although I didn't know it, we were ahead of the Dutch bike by a fraction of a second, but I knew it felt good.

The interesting thing about the kilo is that because it lasts about 60 seconds, and because you have to work so hard to get the heavy bike up to speed, you inevitably fade off towards the end of the race. It's often the tandem that fades the least at the end of the race which is victorious. Perhaps slightly earlier than expected, about 375m into the 1000m race, my legs began registering the tell-tale signs, a feeling of your legs simply not responding. They feel progressively weaker as the various energy systems burn up and disappear, much like a rocket jettisoning its boosters. It's not until the race is over that the huge lactic acid hit comes. 'It's OK, I've planned for this; I've trained for this; it's all about keeping my technique smooth, keeping deceleration to a minimum', I reasoned with myself.

The final lap felt like a war of attrition. We fought our way to the finish line as smoothly as we could to maintain our speed. I gasped for as much oxygen as I could, trying desperately to repay the debt to my now feeble muscles. As we rolled under the giant scoreboard, and I glanced up to see where we'd finished, I was hoping against hope it was enough to take gold. Next to my name was the number that would decide my future. Two. 'We finished second?' I tried to get my head around this as I stared down at the track. I couldn't bring myself to lift my head up and show my face to the world. The physical pain I felt was excruciating, but psychologically it was like being hit by a truck.

Unable to walk, I was helped from the bike to track centre. I collapsed onto the floor and just lay there. 'You've let yourself down. This was meant to be your day. You've let your teammates down, they expected you to win gold, you were favourite. This is Pete's first Paralympics; he's put his heart and soul into it, and you were meant to win this for him. What about your family? They've spent a fortune coming to watch you. You've let them down; they will be so disappointed in you. And what about those watching back home? This is live on television; how many people have seen you fail? You've let them all down, you were meant to win. You told the whole country that you expected to win gold in that bloody interview. You've let your whole nation down. You're a disgrace, you're pathetic!'

Some failures are harder to take than others, a silver medal at a Paralympics may sound like an incredible achievement, but at the time it seemed like the biggest failure of all. It took a while for me to learn the lessons – there were many. Firstly, we got our taper wrong – taper is the training to deliver the best performance at the best time. We were absolutely flying in training two weeks earlier. Had the race happened then, I suspect we might have gone faster. The experience also helped me realise that I needed more in my life. Ultimately it led to me writing this book.

TAKE ACTION

Try to see failure as a win.

- If you fail, you've reached your limit at something. You can alter your strategy and make progress in that area.
- Covering up failures is cheating yourself; you're missing the opportunity to learn and grow.
- Set challenges where failure is a possibility. Seek it out, push your boundaries.

If like me you fail big, look for the lessons to be learned. After every major defeat I've come back faster, stronger and smarter than before. You will too.

Summary

We have completed Stripe Two: Performance. We've looked at how to set and work towards your end goal. We've looked at devising a strategy that challenges you, one that is adaptable. We've looked at how to use lifestyle and environmental improvements to benefit your overall performance. We've considered the importance of tracking your progress and creating accountability. Finally, we've opened ourselves to the idea that failure is something we want, it's what allows us to develop and grow as we work towards our goal.

Stripe Three: The Team

Do you ever have the feeling that when something good happens, you always find a way to mess it up? The problem is that our bodies – particularly our minds – end up in a groove. When our situation changes, we subconsciously react by trying to get back to our old groove. This is self-sabotage. Our subconscious sees the groove as being safe and wants to bring things back there. Think about those lottery winners who end up blowing it all or dieters who put the weight they lost back on.

There is a way to ease your transition to a more fruitful life, a way to avoid sabotaging your potential success. It concerns the company that you keep. What happens is that you gradually adapt to the group of people that you are with. You probably behave very differently with different groups of friends. It therefore stands to reason that when you surround yourself with negative people, you start moaning and complaining too. Similarly, if you spend your time with people who live and breathe cycling, not only do you learn a lot about cycling, you probably also start talking about it.

Surrounded by success

American entrepreneur and motivational speaker Jim Rohn summed it up, 'You are the average of the five people you spend most time with.'[12] He believed that to be successful, you need to surround yourself with successful people. Not that I am suggesting a complete revamp of your social circle. I appreciate that you probably don't want to give up on your current friends. Instead of heading to the pub with them every evening, consider doing something new now and again. Consider where the people you want to emulate are going to be. It could be at a networking event or conference – where you meet people who are either at a similar level to you, or better still, are where you aspire to be.

When you surround yourself with people who are positive and ambitious, you find your motivation increases rapidly. When you tell them about your ideas for success, they don't look for reasons for you to fail. Instead

---

12 Jim Rohn, '7 Tips For Developing Your Personal Philosophy' (2017), www.jimrohn.com/personal-philosophy

they usually give you support or advice to help you on your journey. If they don't think your plans will work, they are more likely to tell you in a constructive way. It appears to be human nature for your current group of friends and family to want to keep you the way you are. This is the norm and therefore safe. It's why they can be negative about your great plans for success. They may also find your transition challenging at times. I can assure you that it will be worth it and when they get used to the new you, they will acknowledge that you made the right call.

If you feel stuck in a rut, it might be necessary to change your environment, and hence the people around you. My massive change came in 2009 when I moved to Manchester to join the British Cycling team. Little did I know how much it would change my own outlook and approach to life.

November 2007: another cold training session in Aberdeen. I went through my usual warm-up routine. I say warm-up, but it was bloody freezing, despite being layered to a point where my movement was slightly restricted and not ideal for running. The athletics stadium stood within walking distance of the North Sea, the stand looked out onto the track, the links golf course and the sea beyond. Absolutely beautiful on a warm, sunny day: this was neither. Instead it was another blustery day with the wind whipping off the sea. It was a challenging place to train in the run-up to a Paralympic Games.

It was another session where I was on my own. My coach Eddie McKenna attended as often as he could, but he was a volunteer. His full-time job as a Church of Scotland minister meant he had many commitments. His dedication to the sport was immense and I could see the strain it was having on his working life. There were other members in my training group, but none were full-time athletes. They didn't have the same dedication and their attendance was pretty hit-and-miss. Not that I held it against them, this was their hobby. They probably had more enjoyable things to do on a cold November day.

I kept looking at the gate, desperate for someone to walk in; I wasn't sure I could face another training session on my own. The enjoyment I got from training had started to slip. I'd always considered myself a good self-motivator, but it's so much easier to motivate yourself on good days. Having someone by your side, experiencing the hardships with you, makes a huge difference. Full-time sport wasn't proving all it was cracked up to be. The athletics track seemed pretty bleak; I only had the grey winter sky to watch over me.

June 2009: I'd been in Manchester for two days. I woke up early, it was my first full training day at the National Cycling Centre. As someone who constantly worries about every small detail, as well as a keen advocate of punctuality, I left early. Despite not being familiar with the route from my newly rented flat to the velodrome, I seemed to get there in record time. I arrived early, ridiculously early. With over an hour and a half until my session started, I took the opportunity to familiarise myself with the venue. The corridors were lined with pictures of every medal winner from the 2008 Beijing Olympic and Paralympic Games. 'What I would give to have my photo on that wall,' I thought.

Time suitably killed, I changed and made my way into the track centre. I'd been told this is where everyone gathered for training. I felt rather awkward as I sat down. Here I was on my own again: memories of my lonely sessions in the Aberdeen stadium flooded back. As the start of the training time approached, members of the squad arrived. I looked up and was shocked to see people I recognised. Walking towards me were Olympic Champions Jason Kenny, Victoria Pendleton and Chris Hoy.

Although I was awe-struck, I did my best to look cool by fiddling with my cycling helmet. I'd been on training camps with some impressive people during my athletics days, but this was different. I had watched these guys on television, shouting and cheering them to glory. As they approached, I returned to my helmet. 'Afternoon,' said Chris. I looked up. 'Nobody else here,' I thought. Chris held his hand out for me to shake. 'He's talking to you, Neil, say something.' 'Hi,' I replied bravely. I was fortunate enough to have met Chris once before. The evening before the taster session, I had attended an event in Manchester for athletes returning from the Olympics and Paralympics. By chance, I found myself sitting next to Chris and I took the opportunity to ask for some cycling tips for my first go on the velodrome.

Chris being Chris remembered it. 'So, I take it the trial went well?' I laughed and updated him on my cycling journey. Despite his huge success, bear in mind that he was reigning BBC Sports Personality of the Year, Chris is one of the most down-to-earth people you will ever meet. He doesn't talk about himself but jumps in with questions about you. He is an outstanding example of how you can be both successful and humble.

The training session got underway and between each stint we returned to the track centre to rest. During this time-out the riders would talk to one another, either about cycling or life in general. I got chatting to Vicky Pendleton, she asked how I was settling in. When she heard about my lack of cooking skills, she gave me a recipe for a simple chicken dish that would be a tasty, healthy option. I was blown away by this environment, training alongside people who were immensely successful. I was spending quality time with people who were achieving the things I wanted to achieve. Not only did I have the opportunity to train with them, they also wanted to talk to me and offer advice and support.

Right from my first day at British Cycling I found something that was lacking during my lonely training in Aberdeen. I found like-minded people who understood what I was going through. People I could share my experiences with and who could offer advice on how to overcome the inevitable challenges I would encounter. Over the following months, I became acutely aware of how powerful this was, my performance on the bike began to skyrocket. I learnt that if you put yourself in the right environment and surrounded yourself with the right people, you are capable of seriously improving your performance. Remember Jim Rohn's saying, 'You are the average of the five people you spend most time with.' Choose your five wisely.

TAKE ACTION

Consider the five people you spend most time with.

- Are they conducive to your success? If not, could you branch out and meet new people?
- Where do the people you want to be like gather?
- Consider spending less time with those who bring you down
- Find people who will help you grow

If you feel uncomfortable about this, bear in mind that it's your brain trying to maintain the status quo and keep you in your groove. Be aware that this is self-sabotage and try to avoid it.

Asking for help

'No, sorry, I've got training tonight.'

'Well, what about after training?'

'No, I'll be late back.'

Training was always a good excuse. I managed to avoid another opportunity to socialise with my friends. Naturally, they didn't bother asking again. By sixteen, my social circle was becoming increasingly small. It wasn't because I didn't want to go out. I enjoyed hanging out with friends, trying to attract girls. Mind you, I'd given up asking girls out. That old technique of asking, 'Will you go out with me?' before running away, didn't produce great results. So, I'd shelved it. 'Let them come to you,' I decided. They never did.

The truth is I was scared. Most people were unaware of my visual impairment. In fairness, I hid it pretty well. After meetings with my teachers, I was placed at the front of the class for most of my lessons. As well as struggling to see small things, I was short-sighted. This meant I could just about see the black- and whiteboards. They also wanted me to use enlarged text for my exams. 'What will everyone think of me?' I worried. My biggest challenge, though, was my lack of sight when light levels were low. Although it was OK most of the time, the school corridors were really dull, and I often didn't recognise people. It's really embarrassing when people say hello and you can't tell who they are or whether they're even talking to you. After a cringe-worthy incident when I replied to a question that someone had asked their friend, not me, I opted for the not-smiling or waving-back approach. Unsurprisingly, people thought I was anti-social.

The dining hall was my nightmare; something I'd re-experience at the Paralympic Games. How does anyone find their friends in these places? I would walk towards the rows of tables with my tray, desperately hoping I might recognise one of the blurs sitting in groups and laughing. Was the laughter aimed at me? I began to develop techniques. Always enter the canteen with someone you know. Make sure you are ahead of them in the queue so that you order first. Then wait for them and follow them to a seat. As my social circle decreased, there were days when I had to enter the canteen alone. I would buy something quick and easy to eat, like a slice of pizza. If I couldn't find a seat that was on its own, I'd eat standing up and make my escape as quickly as possible.

In Aberdeen it gets dark incredibly early in the winter. It was often dark when I got out of school. I'd been provided with a taxi pick-up during the winter for a couple of years. I convinced a few people that it was because I lived far away, but as I arranged to be picked up long after everyone had left the school grounds, most were completely unaware. My best friend Graham would generally wait with me. He was aware I had a condition but didn't realise how bad it was until years later. I joked that I was forced to take the taxi because of protocol and I'd only agreed because it meant I wouldn't have to walk. I imagined he'd think I was cooler if I played the system. It would have been torture walking home in the dark with my friends from school and have them see me struggle.

Fitting in at school was so important. What would people think of me if they knew I couldn't see very well? 'My life wouldn't be worth living,' I reasoned. I preferred to spend another evening alone; fortunately, I learnt to enjoy my own company. 'I'm not missing out anyway, they'll just be talking about their driving lessons. Then I'll have to dodge the obvious questions.' Not being able to drive was one of my major frustrations.

Fast forward six years to November 2006. It was a few months since my first Athletics World Championships. A chat with my coach Eddie developed into a deep discussion. Something he said that day has stuck with me, 'Now that you are involved in disability sport, you need to start accepting that you are considered disabled.' I was surprised that he thought that I didn't consider myself disabled. Eddie had planted a seed. I realised that I had never accepted my disability and I still tried to hide it from people. I'd much rather struggle on my own or shy away from situations.

We continued to discuss my training plan for the winter months. There was a problem. My usual training track was due to close while the facility was upgraded. We would have to train on grass fields in the city. There would be no floodlights. I became fixated, trapped between a rock and a hard place. How was I going to run at full speed in the dark with no vision? Equally, I couldn't not train, the Paralympics were my dream. My stress levels rocketed until I admitted there might be an issue. I was nervous, 'I'm going to struggle to run in the dark, I can't see too well when the light level is low. Actually, I can't see at all.' 'I know,' replied Eddie. Once it was out in the open, we began brainstorming ideas. We explored whether there were other floodlit facilities; nothing was available with the regularity that we needed. Eventually – with my permission – we opened the problem up to my training group. Within a few minutes, one of my training partners came up with an ingenious idea. 'What if you were to set up a series of lights along the ground? Basically, you follow the lights.'

Trial day was a week later. We sourced small lights that could be laid on the ground. Placing them in pairs every 10 metres or so, we essentially created a runway for me to run through. A car was positioned by the track with its headlights blazing so I could see where to start. I was nervous, I looked up at the string of lights in front of me. It was literally all I could see. I would be sprinting as fast as I could into the abyss.

Having a goal that meant more to me than the perceived embarrassment of others knowing the truth, had allowed me to open up and reach out for help. The way my team had rallied around to come up with a solution in my time of need was incredible. It was then that I began to realise that I was stronger when I asked for help. Struggling on by myself had its limitations; allowing others to help ultimately led to my Paralympic qualification. I had stepped way out of my comfort zone and another challenge had been overcome.

This is just one example of how I have benefited when asking for help. I'm always surprised how people rally round to come up with highly effective solutions in my hour of need. Being able to get a fresh perspective on your situation can be invaluable. We are often guilty of thinking we are stronger by doing something by ourselves. As though by asking someone to give us a hand, we are weak. It's still something I struggle with from time to time, particularly when asking for directions. I'm not sure whether this is a male thing. I often regarded my disability as a weakness, in reality it was my ego that was holding me back.

If you're going to reach the top, you won't be doing it alone. I can guarantee that. Don't be afraid to ask for help from those around you. The quickest and easiest way to learn is by talking to people who are where you want to be. Once I joined British Cycling, this meant talking to athletes who had achieved success. If you can find yourself a mentor in the field you aim to succeed in, your level of progression will significantly increase. I can't stress enough how rapid your success can be if you are able to learn from someone who's been there, done it and made the mistakes you will inevitably make. It's a lesson I've certainly learnt during my time in sport and I am eternally grateful to those who have helped me along the way. I've never had one specific mentor figure in my life, rather there has been a collection of people. Eddie is one of them. By challenging me to face reality and look at things from another perspective, he opened up a world of possibilities for me. Since then I've become more accepting of my disability, though this may always remain a work in progress.

Try not to appear different, fit in with the crowd and just struggle on. Does this sound like your typical successful person? Far from it. People don't remember those who just fit in with the crowd. It's the ones who dared to be different that we remember, the ones who leave their mark on history. It's time to swallow your pride and ask for advice from people who know more than you.

TAKE ACTION

Lose the ego. You can't do it alone, no matter how strong and capable you are.

- Accept you have limitations, accept the help of others and excel. You will face many challenges, attack them with all you have, but if someone's help will make the task easier, don't let that opportunity pass you by.

- Consider finding a mentor figure. Most people are willing to help others; it's in our nature to find helping others rewarding. Approach someone who is already where you want to be. Buy them coffee and get chatting, ask questions, learn.

Remember that social media allows you to build up relationships with people you might think are unreachable.

Your team

'Be self-sustainable, they'll respect you for that. The mark of a true champion is someone who can get to the top without needing help. You've made it this far on your own.' This was my way of thinking. I was at my first training camp with British Athletics in late 2005. Reluctantly, I was assessed by a physiotherapist, which is standard protocol for new athletes joining the programme. The feedback from the assessment was fairly substantial. 'There are several reasons why you are having to deal with this constant back pain, tight hamstrings and achy knees.' I asked whether it was not just general training pain.

I was advised to see a physiotherapist when I returned to Aberdeen. We began a programme to sort my posture out, it was a slow and sometimes arduous process.

The physio asked me about my lifting technique in the gym. My response resulted in me being sent to see a strength and conditioning coach, as well as a podiatrist to ensure my feet were in the correct position. Before I knew it, I had visited several specialists. It took time, but my back pain disappeared, I started lifting more weights in the gym, and crucially I got faster on the track. 'Maybe there is something in this after all,' I thought.

My early experiences in athletics taught me that I could attain a far higher level if I used the knowledge of experts. But it wasn't until I joined British Cycling that I witnessed the power of a centralised team of experts. British Cycling is based at the National Cycling Centre in Manchester. For most of the national cycling disciplines, you are expected to base yourself in the Manchester area, training and working with the support staff at the venue.

This wasn't the case during my athletics career, I was based in Aberdeen and my teammates were dotted all over the country. It meant that I would see a specialist in my local area, and they would see someone in theirs. The beauty of having a centralised system is that everyone can access the same group of specialists. It benefits both the athletes and staff. By having access to elite riders who specialise in a specific discipline, the specialists in turn become even more niche by treating similar problems. This develops a unique learning effect where everyone's knowledge becomes increasingly refined. As a team, we can drill down to the finest of details, finding previously unattainable gains in performance.

By the time I walk towards the start line at a Paralympic Games, over the course of the previous four years I will have worked with a multitude of specialists at British Cycling. These include coaches, physiotherapists, physiologists, performance analysts, bio mechanists, nutritionists, psychologists, lifestyle advisors, performance directors and many more. You come to realise that to learn all the skills you require to make it to the top is a fruitless pursuit. There simply aren't enough hours in the day. Instead, by using experts in their field, you can achieve more success with less effort.

Imagine building your success to be like building a house. When there are little jobs to be done, you might tackle some DIY. Nothing too fancy; perhaps re-attach a cupboard door that's fallen off. DIY is all well and good if you have the time and it's something relatively easy to fix. When it comes to building a house, the last thing you want to do is to build it yourself from scratch. It wouldn't make sense. Although you may grasp the basic principles of bricklaying, plumbing and wiring, you know that there are people who are trained in these skills. Unless you suffer from a particularly large ego, you recognise they will do a far better job. In order to create the best house, you need specialists. Why should building your success be any different? Your architect in this case would be a coach or mentor. Someone you can discuss your plan with and who isn't afraid to tell you when you deviate from it.

I create my initial plan by sitting down with my coach one to one. We look at what we hope to achieve over the next one to four years, depending on where we are in the four-year Paralympic Games cycle. We discuss my ultimate goal and how we plan to achieve it. Once we are both clear on the overall plan, we meet with the rest of my team to work out the finer details.

I strongly recommend that you find a coach or mentor and go through this process. Although it can be done on your own, having a different perspective always helps. Family and friends may suffice, but you need to be wary. Anyone who is emotionally attached to you might find it difficult to point out your shortcomings, or conversely, they might try to tell you not to chase your dreams. It is human nature to protect those you care about either from short-term discomfort, such as a few home truths, or from long-term pain, in terms of potential failure. Also, loved ones may not want to see you succeed because they are worried that success might change you.

I trust my team to provide me with the best knowledge and support they can. I talk to them about my overall goals, so that they buy into them too. If they know what I need overall, it lets them understand what other members of my team are doing and how the whole puzzle fits together. Once we are all aligned and working towards the same goal, things run at a much higher level and facilitate peak performance.

TAKE ACTION

Begin by deciding on the skills and expertise you need and then build a team around you. In my business, I use graphic designers, filmmakers, marketing specialists and publishers. This gives me the freedom to spend time doing what I do best, working with clients.

Consider how you might create your team.

- It could be people you work with directly, or individual specialists for specific tasks.
- To be a success at what you do, you need time to dedicate to the things you do best. Having someone to take care of any other issues will free up your time.
- Trusting specialists to do a better job than you will result in higher quality output.

Remember that time is your most valuable asset, anything you can do to free up time is to your advantage.

Communication

Working in a team has its challenges. Everyone reacts differently to different scenarios and being in a tense group environment can be daunting. Some people find it immensely challenging to get their point across, preferring to take a back seat. For many years that was me. My lack of confidence in my teenage years meant I struggled in social situations. I lacked conviction in what I said. Sport gave me the self-confidence to talk to people, but the idea of speaking out in a group situation was a complete no-go.

Although there are flaws in the education system, one thing I am grateful for is that during my school years I was required to stand up in front of the class and give a talk. Mind you, I wouldn't have said it at the time and looking back I wish there had been more opportunities. I would worry for days in advance and during the talk I would sound nervous and sway from side to side. I fear my performance would be best described as 'tedious'.

The feedback I received was often along the lines, 'Great content, expertly researched, but need to work on presentation skills.' When communication and the ability to articulate are so integral to how you perform in life, it baffles me why the education system doesn't place more importance on it. Many people rank public speaking as one of their highest fears; I think this is due to lack of practice.

Once I became a full-time athlete, I had a few opportunities to talk to an audience about my sporting career. It initially involved speaking to employees at golfing days for local companies who supported me financially. I would like to take this opportunity to apologise to anyone who had to listen to those initial performances. A brief and rapid run-down of my sporting career was pretty much it. Crucially, it was the starting point to my public speaking career. It also made me realise that nothing awful was going to happen by getting up there and saying a few words. In fact, a lot of people seemed genuinely interested to hear from me. As I became more successful, opportunities became more regular; with practice I became far more comfortable at speaking. This isn't to say I don't get nervous beforehand. It's the same with racing, a part of my brain tells me that I'd rather not be there, it would be much easier to walk away. This feeling is always dwarfed by the buzz I get from being on stage and sharing my message. In fact, public speaking is probably the closest thing I can find to racing when it comes to the adrenaline rush. It might not quite be to the same degree, but there is always a level of exhilaration if a speaking gig has gone well.

Over time I began to develop my story, adding a dash of humour and a touch of showmanship. It turned into a performance rather than a talk. I was learning how to communicate with progressively larger rooms of people, and I was enjoying it more each time. The ability to articulate oneself, to express thoughts in a succinct way, is a skill that is learnt. I noticed that I was becoming more confident and this was starting to influence how I behaved in team meetings. Rather than sitting back and letting everyone else do the talking, I became more confident in expressing my opinions. The overall result was a meeting tailored more towards my needs as an athlete.

This brings us on nicely to effective communication in a team. Something widely used within elite sport, as well as in the armed forces and medicine, is debriefing. Athletes are very good at analysing their own performances, it's a skill I have developed over the years without realising. It wasn't until I learnt how to communicate effectively that I was able to bring this self-analysis into a team environment. Debriefing is an immensely powerful tool that helps a team understand what happened, why it happened and what lessons can be learnt going forward. In the previous chapter we looked at creating your strategy. We discussed how it constantly evolves, debriefing is how we discover where and how it must evolve.

I use two types of debriefing – hot and cold debriefs. Hot debriefs take place soon after the event has taken place. For me this is generally after a race or training session. In a race scenario it usually involves me, my pilot and my coach sitting down and talking it out. When required we bring in a performance analyst or physiotherapist. Emotional responses are encouraged, it helps us to process what has happened, but crucially it's a safe place where criticism is kept to a minimum. By talking about the race, we all remember small details that happened during the race itself, we can talk about what worked well and where we could have improved.

Any action points can then be targeted. The debrief takes place whether we win or lose. It's obvious to pick holes in something that hasn't gone well, but there are countless lessons to be learnt from successes, too.

After a few days we perform a cold debrief. It's a far more logical and detached run-down. We only include necessary data, this could be times or video analysis, that might add to our analysis of what happened. After a few days' reflection, these discussions often throw up different things from the hot debrief. It gives us the opportunity to seriously consider where improvements can be made, as well as brainstorm how we should alter our overall strategy in line with our findings.

A solid debriefing strategy is integral to the success of an athlete and it's something I teach my clients to implement. Some feel that it sounds too time-consuming, a process they can't afford to add to their already busy schedules. Once they realise how quick and effective a debrief can be, they always seem to get huge benefit from it. Lessons are learnt, strategies are altered, and performance improvements are identified.

Don't underestimate the importance of being able to communicate well if you are to succeed. It is in everything you do. It is often something we take for granted and don't necessarily consider it as a skill that can be developed. Like everything, there is always room for improvement. Develop your communication skills, implement hot and cold debriefs and watch your performance blossom.

TAKE ACTION

The ideal way to improve your communication skills is to get out there and start talking. I am a strong advocate for public speaking. Those who are willing to step out of their comfort zone are the ones who reap the rewards.

You might ask, 'Who wants to hear me talk? What do I have to say?' Regardless of who you are and what you do, you have knowledge and experiences to share:

- What have you learnt to get to this point in your life?
- What skills have you picked up that other people might not have?

The next step is to go online and search for groups that meet in your area and get in touch. They could be specific speaking groups, business groups or local community groups.

Even if your presentation is only five minutes, it's a starting point. Start to develop your skills and your story. Your timing, content and delivery will all improve. These skills can translate into something you can use during meetings, discussions or one-to-one chats with your team.

Implement debriefing after major events. This could include the completion of a project, a presentation or a meeting with a client. The debrief should take place in two parts, the hot and cold elements.

Hot debrief: This should take place straight after the event. Emotions are encouraged, all opinions are welcome and all member of the debrief carry equal weight. Seniority is not welcome in this environment. Ask the questions:

- What were we trying to accomplish?
- What have we done well/not well?
- What were the outcomes of our actions?
- What should we continue to do and what needs changing?

Ensure any action points are noted and dealt with.

Cold debrief: This should happen two to five days after the event. Any useful data or information should be brought to the debrief. This meeting is more forensic. The extra reflection time after the event might throw up different opinions. Ask the same questions as above and note any action points.

Remember, if debriefing is good enough for sport, medicine and the armed forces, it's good for business, too.

Teamwork for performance

Once your team is in place, you need to find the best way to work together and get the most out of each other. In your drive for success, it's easy to slip into a dog-eat-dog mindset. This only gets you so far and is more likely to cause you to crash and burn. Many of today's most prosperous companies are changing the way they do business. They have realised that their employees are not commodities to be worked to the bone and tossed onto the scrap heap, ready to bring in the next batch. Instead, they work with their employees to get the best out of them. Many companies have found that affording their employees a level of autonomy, in other words, the freedom to approach tasks in the manner they think best, dramatically increases team performance.

Most importantly of all, they have realised that to get results, they need employees to buy into their purpose. A shared drive is an immensely powerful tool. A shared purpose can make a team forego personal short-term success in favour of the long-term success of the whole team. In other words, sacrifice yourself for the team.

You can see this 'sacrifice for the team' in many sports, but perhaps it's most evident in the New Zealand rugby team. There has been much discussion about the work ethic and team dynamics of the All Blacks. In James Kerr's book, *Legacy*,[13] he describes the squad ethos. A few of the players decided to create a set of guidelines, the *Black Book*, that outlined the principles that All Blacks must adhere to. Each player received a copy and was expected to not only live by these guidelines,

---

13   James Kerr, *Legacy* (Constable, 2013)

but also hold their teammates accountable. Two of the principles really stood out:

1. No one is bigger than the team

2. Leave the jersey in a better place

We often hear about teams that are better than the sum of their parts. I usually find this refers to lesser teams performing above expectations. We rarely hear it said about teams that are performing at their pinnacle. This is probably because, as spectators, we tend to focus on the star players. However, when it comes to the All Blacks, we see a team that is stronger than the sum of its parts. There's no doubt that the team is full of global stars, but by dropping their egos and putting everything on the line for the whole team, the outcome is awe-inspiring. In 2020, the All Blacks win percentage stood at a staggering 77.41% since their first test match in 1903.[14] Despite stars coming and going, the team just keeps on winning.

The players genuinely seem humble. Despite their immense achievements, they all recognise that the team is bigger than them. A team that functions this way will pull together when the times are tough and won't get complacent when the going is good. They will always strive to be the best they can for the sake of the team.

---

14   All Blacks, www.allblacks.com/teams/all-blacks

That's where the next principle comes in. Leave the jersey in a better place. When a new All Black is presented with their game jersey, they are told to leave the jersey in a better place. In other words, they need to pick up from where the last guy to wear their number left off and take it to another level. The thinking behind this principle is that you must *always* strive to be the best you can, both on and off the field, for the good of the team.

I try to adopt this principle when I represent my country. The day you receive the official kit with Great Britain emblazoned on it is unforgettable. For me, it was when I was in athletics. I am still as proud to put on my British Cycling jersey to this day. There is a great sense of responsibility when you represent your nation. It's no longer just about you. You feel part of something bigger. You are buying into a cause and as such you can find something extra. The desire to perform for the good of your team adds to your personal drive. And as we've already discovered, drive is the first step towards success.

You may not be sporting a national jersey every day, but you still represent a team. How can you create a shared purpose? What goal would your team be willing to buy into? I meet with my team to discuss the overall goal – Paralympic gold. As a wider cycling team, we aim to win as many medals as possible. It's something we all want and, as such, the team will do what it can to achieve this collective outcome. Each individual gives up their time to help me when I need it, and I do the same for them. Provided everything we do is directed towards that shared goal, we are happy to dedicate all the time and energy it takes.

One of the best examples of high-pressured teamwork was in the run-up to the 2014 Commonwealth Games. This was my first Commonwealth Games and the first time tandem cycling was part of the schedule. Because a full programme of para events isn't logistically possible, they are integrated into the competition schedule alongside the 'able-bodied' events. It means we are accorded equal status.

Not only was it my first Commonwealth Games and the first time I represented Team Scotland, it was also taking place in Glasgow. The Paralympic Games had been in London just two years previously and here I was again – competing at home on another big stage. Success in Glasgow would mean everything to me. The opportunity to perform in front of a home crowd was both incredibly exciting and incredibly nerve-wracking. I wanted to win, not only for myself and for my team, but also for my country. It was also the chance to show the world how far parasport had come. I wanted to showcase paracycling and excite the crowd.

The pressure I put on myself was intense. But it wasn't just about me, it takes two to tandem. A team of two on a bike, with a wider team behind us, made up of both Team Scotland and British Cycling. I was to ride with Craig Maclean. It was Craig who I bumped into at the Manchester velodrome and launched my career in cycling. I felt I needed to win this for Craig. During our time on the British Cycling team we had raced both together and against each other. Together we won double gold at the 2011 World Championships in Italy, breaking the 200-metre world record. A year later, we raced against each other at both the World Championships and the London 2012 Paralympics.

Here we were back together. I'm sure Craig won't mind me saying, but at Glasgow 2014 it seemed as though he was coming to the end of his career. (Astonishingly, he went on to compete with James Ball at the Rio 2016 Paralympics, finishing fifth.) At the time of Glasgow Games, he was 42 (with his 43rd birthday the following week). Never have I known a 42-year-old man in such tremendous shape. The younger cyclists at British Cycling were in awe of his muscular physique. Along with his athletic ability, Craig also brought experience and a tremendous sense of humour to the squad. Never one to shy away from telling you the harsh truth, he always found a funny way to deliver it, so you could never be annoyed at him.

Despite his age, I knew Craig was more than up to the challenge of targeting gold in Glasgow. The problem was that full-time training for over two decades takes its toll. As such you have to be smart about how you train. For Craig, this meant reducing the amount of training. He found that his performance deteriorated, and his body suffered if he trained hard two days in a row. The quality of his training was exceptional, but he needed much more time between sessions to recover. As I was relatively new to cycling, I benefited from more time on the bike. I needed to be doing specific track sessions at least three times a week, as well as being on the bike five to six days a week. It was obviously a serious conflict of interest for us.

Craig is such a nice guy and was willing to put in the training I needed. As the sighted pilot, he felt it was his responsibility to do as much as he could for his visually impaired partner. It would have been easy for me just to accept this. It meant I would be in the best shape possible. The problem was that me being in the best shape far from guaranteed us winning. Remember, it takes two to tandem. If one person isn't on top form, then the bike as a whole will suffer. I knew that to win gold, both Craig and I had to be in the best shape possible.

I had to make a compromise. We decided to limit our time on the tandem. We would train together once or twice a week. These were high quality sessions. While Craig was resting up and recovering, I would find alternative ways to train. It meant doing more sessions on the turbo trainer (a stand in which a bike can be placed, applying resistance so that it can be used statically), or on a static rig designed to resemble a track bike, with higher gearing and a large flywheel to provide resistance and momentum. Although I was missing out on some technical improvements I could have made from more time on the tandem, physically I still got most of the training I needed. I sacrificed an element of my own performance for the good of the team. It meant that we got to the start line with Craig in one piece.

TAKE ACTION

Consider the overall team performance.

- Even though you might gain respect for being the strongest and most successful member of the team, finding a way to make the whole team more effective is far more impressive.
- A team functions better when it has a shared drive or purpose. Consider your goals and inspire everyone to unite around them.
- A team motto or slogan can be powerful.

Being part of a team can be one of the most rewarding experiences.

Teamwork for success

The Commonwealth Games is an unusual experience, by dividing the United Kingdom into its four nations you end up competing against teammates from the Great Britain team. Equally strange is that the support staff I work with on a daily basis are either split across the different teams or simply not going. This included my coach at the time, Jon Norfolk. Jon was an ex-rider on the GB Olympic squad and had tremendous knowledge and experience. As he had also been a tandem pilot, I was delighted when he was appointed coach. Jon and I shared the same goal, Paralympic success. At times though our personalities clashed, which resulted in a few heated debates over the years. Despite this, I knew that not having my coach at a major championship could be problematic. I was going to have to form new partnerships with members of the Team Scotland staff in one of the most high-pressured situations. One member of Team Scotland was a young sprint coach, Kevin Stewart. Kevin had been a development rider on the GB squad but had left the programme just before I joined. I'd heard a few stories about him but didn't know what to expect.

Craig and I travelled up to Glasgow from Manchester on the English Cycling coach. While they were the 'enemy', they were also the teammates we trained with every day. There were the obvious jokes about whether or not to let us on the bus. When we arrived at the athletes' village, we were met by members of Team Scotland. It felt like an official handover as we transferred from our usual staff team to a completely new environment.

After a brief tour of the village we met up with our fellow Scottish Cycling riders who welcomed us. One or two were on the British Cycling team, but many I'd not met before. They had been training together in the run-up to the Games and spent time in training camps abroad. As Craig and I had remained in Manchester to train, we initially felt like outsiders. However, Craig – somewhat of a legend in Scotland – is such a likeable guy that it didn't take long for everyone to warm to us. We met up with Kevin Stewart to discuss our training needs in the run-up to race day. Kevin is an absolute bear of a man, obviously an ex-sprinter. It wasn't just his physical presence that struck me, this young guy had a real aura of assurance. I instantly knew we could rely on him. From that moment I tipped Kevin to go on to great things: he's now with British Cycling as a senior sprint coach for the Olympic programme.

Craig and I headed to the velodrome to see how it was kitted out for the Games and to meet the mechanics, managers and helpers. Tandems are notoriously tricky bikes; it was important to spend time with the mechanics so they were comfortable with our bike and knew our requirements. We also had to strike up a relationship with the other staff members. They would be providing us with everything we needed to give our best performance. The Sir Chris Hoy Velodrome looked immaculate, we had ridden it before, but now that it was Games ready it had a different feel. Excitement and nerves were starting to ramp up.

The days in the run-up to race day were long and slow. I was becoming increasingly aware from press and social media coverage that we were the hotly tipped gold medal contenders for Team Scotland. The home nation was eager for success and racing on days two and three meant we had the chance to set the tone for the wider team. Though if things didn't go to plan, how might that impact on everyone else? Our media officer Jay told us we would attract a lot of media hype. She would minimise our exposure to it on our first race day. We would only have to carry out post-race interviews at the venue. If things went well after our second event it was likely we'd be asked to do a television and radio tour. I had really been looking forward to the Commonwealth Games, but now I was wondering whether I wanted to put myself on the line with a whole nation watching, expecting.

After the official team photo, the cyclists headed back to our accommodation to watch the opening ceremony on television. As we were nearly all racing in the next few days, the squad decided not to attend the ceremony. When we heard the BBC mention Craig and I as potential home nation gold medal contenders, a cheer went up and I took a deep breath.

I spent much of day one in our house watching the track cycling on my iPad; it was just a few hundred metres away from the velodrome. My British Cycling tandem teammates Sophie Thornhill and Helen Scott took gold for England in the sprint. Silver was won by ex-GB and current Team Scotland teammates Aileen McGlynn and Louise Haston. Tandem racing was making its debut at these Games and the fans loved it. A home silver medal was a fantastic start for us, and I was delighted for my English teammates. Tomorrow would be our turn. That night would be sleepless.

The one-kilometre time trial was due to start at 16.11 which meant I had time to kill. I spent a lot of time wondering how big a threat our Australian opponents would be. We were going head-to-head with para-cycling legend Kieran Modra piloted by Jason Niblett, former member of the Australian cycling team and gold medal winner from the previous Commonwealth Games in the team sprint. They were a significant threat. Pete Mitchell and I had managed to pip them in both events at the World Championships earlier that year when they were still a relatively new pairing. Now they had spent more time together, I knew they would be fast. I tried to keep my nerves under control by working through the plan I'd written down. Because my stomach was churning, I ate meals out of necessity rather than enjoyment.

It was time to head to the velodrome. During the warm-up, people started flooding into the stadium; I became more aware of the magnitude of the situation. The noise was building, and I could see plenty of Scottish flags. As current World Champion, I would be last to go in the four-lap race. I watched as the Welsh, Northern Irish and second Australian bike all rode solid times, but nothing to be nervous about.

Last to go before us were Kieran and Jason. They recorded a time of 62.244 seconds. The fastest Craig and I had ridden was 62.6 at the World Championships in 2011. This was going to be a big ask. Craig and I are sprinters – we go out very fast and then fade badly at the finish. We knew the only way we could win was by getting a huge lead early on. We attacked the start with everything we had; in the opening lap we had a substantial lead of 0.766 seconds. By the end of lap two the gap had grown to 1.091 seconds. Although we were starting to fade, we still held a lead of 0.953 seconds with one lap to go. It felt as though the wheels began to fall off. I could feel the bike decelerating and feared the worst. Desperately fighting to reach the finish line we ran over one of the foam markers, causing us to lose more speed. We lunged for the line and heard a collective gasp from the frantic crowd. A deafening roar followed. 0.148 seconds separated us from the Australians; crucially it was in our favour. I held my arms aloft and soaked up the atmosphere. We were Commonwealth Champions. We had won on home soil. I was overjoyed and, perhaps even more, relieved.

Craig and I sang the anthem with pride. No more did I want to be the guy who didn't sing. My voice cracked a few times, but the crowd made up for it by singing with gusto. There were countless interviews for live television and radio, as well as the national press. Cameras flashed and congratulations poured in. We did our best to enjoy it but knew the following morning we'd be back on track racing. We made our way back to our Team Scotland house and tried to rest. I spent most of the evening on social media, before another restless night.

The next day I was aware of how awful my legs felt. Sprint day involves a qualifying ride plus a number of races throughout the day. This could go one of two ways. The discomfort in my legs might ease and they'd feel stronger as the day went on, or the fatigue might just continue to increase.

The qualifying ride, the flying 200m, was average. Again, we were last to go, but our time of 10.213 seconds didn't come close to the Australian pair who clocked a sea level world record equalling 10.050 seconds. We were racing the Welsh bike in the best of three semi-finals. I was feeling rough, my legs were burning, and the exertion was making my stomach turn. The velo-drome felt incredibly hot and I was trying to look as strong as I could, I didn't want my competitors to know how weak I felt. Craig and I battled past the Welsh pair two nil, safely into the finals against the Australians. The finals would take place in the afternoon; we made our way back to the house to rest. A brief nap and food helped, but I still wasn't confident. I was so worried about letting the nation down that I sent out a tweet in the hope it might ease the level of expectation. 'Safely into the gold medal ride-off later this afternoon. Odds are against us, but isn't that what being Scottish is all about? #BringItOn.'

It was time to battle for gold in the best of three. Two bikes, four men, all desperate to succeed. The Australians wanted revenge for the previous day's defeat, and we wanted victory for the incredible fans. Heart pounding the race began. The Australians were leading out and the race was cagey to begin with. Two and a half laps to go and we decided to attack. The Australians matched our pace and we were stuck on the outside. Craig decided to swing up the track for another attack. The gap increased and we didn't have the legs to get back alongside. We were one nil down and comfortably beaten. Before the second ride Craig and I had a quick chat about tactics. 'Look, I don't see how we can beat them, let's just make them do all the work and wait until the home straight to try to get alongside them. It's unlikely we'll get by, but at least we won't look like idiots,' said Craig. 'Yeah, I agree, they're so strong, let's just make it a good race,' I replied. 'We need to make sure they ride hard from a way out, so I'll shout for you to sprint a few times. Don't go though, it's just a dummy. Hopefully they'll hear and think we're attacking.' We had a plan – not a great one – but a plan.

The race began and the first issue, given that we had to lead out, was how to get the Australians out front, entice them to attack. Riding slowly, they took the bait with three and a half laps to go. Time to put Craig's plan into action. 'Up!' he shouted. The Australians accelerated. We sat right behind them, enjoying the reduced air friction to ride through. Another shout and again they accelerated. So far so good, they were working hard, and we were hanging on. We entered the final lap and they kicked with everything they had left, going for gold. We dug deep and, slowly but surely, pulled back towards them. As we entered the final bend, we reached their rear wheel. The gap stayed constant around the bend, which meant that as we entered the home straight, we were still a tandem bike length down with just metres to go. Hammering the pedals as hard as we could, we pulled alongside them, before a final lunge. Incredibly our wheel crossed the line first. It was one all. The noise in the velodrome was insane. Everyone had jumped to their feet, roaring with delight. I was physically and mentally exhausted: I doubted we could do it again.

Craig was laughing. 'Same plan?' he asked.

'Hell yeah, one more time.'

The decider was just a few minutes away. I tried to get as much oxygen into my burning muscles as I could.

The final ride began with the Australians in front. They were keen to ride a slow tactical race. We encouraged them to pick up the pace by taking height on the track and weaving around in fake attacks. They weren't reacting and maintained their tactical approach. With two laps to go, the pace started to creep up and we tucked in. Still no sign of attack as the bell signalled the final lap. With three quarters of a lap to go we accelerated with everything we had left. To my surprise we flew alongside the Australians and passed them. They tried to fight back but had nothing left. It hadn't occurred to me that they might be even more tired than me. We reached the finish line and I raised both arms to the sky. It was double gold and the Glasgow velodrome was rocking. I pointed at the crowd and applauded, I felt as though they'd won it for us. Where there are Scots, there's The Proclaimers. The loudspeaker blared out *I'm Gonna Be* and the crowd joined in. So did I as I held the Scottish Saltire aloft on the back of the tandem. It is an incredible memory. We found our families in the stands and relished the moment. My nephew Logan gave me a huge hug as I handed the flag to him. It was wonderful to share this moment with my family.

After seemingly endless interviews, we made our way to the Scottish pit area to thank the staff. This team we'd spent so little time with had done an incredible job. We'd explained what we needed from them and had trusted them to deliver. They had done exactly that. Although two men stood atop that podium, it was a team who stood with us. As Jay our media officer had predicted, we were in demand that night. Among the many highlights, we appeared live on BBC with Gary Lineker and on The Clare Balding Show. During the following days we travelled around Glasgow, signing autographs and posing for photographs. The city was alive, and our nation was proud of us. I doubt there will be another moment like that in my career – thank you, Glasgow.

Teamwork was crucial to our success. Forming relationships and communicating clearly what we needed were
vital. However, we wouldn't have won gold without
the hot debrief Craig and I held after the defeat in the
first ride of the finals. With just a few minutes to come
up with something, we devised a plan that turned a
losing situation into a winning one.

TAKE ACTION

Be clear what you expect from people and what you
need from them.

- In high-pressure situations, you have to rely on
  others and sometimes they are people you've never
  worked with.
- Give them the autonomy to deal with the situation
  in their own way, but make sure you share the same
  outcomes.
- Use your new-found debriefing skills to transform a
  losing situation into a winning one. It takes clear-cut
  communication and trust.

If you can adjust your strategy in high-stress situations,
you will have the agility to stay ahead.

Summary

Congratulations on completing Stripe Three: The Team.
We've looked at how you can and should build a team

of experts around you. Using people who excel at what they do means that you can concentrate on what you do best. Debrief with those individuals after key phases, note what lessons can be learnt, and use it to adapt your strategy. If possible, seek out a mentor figure to guide you on your journey.

In the next stripe we look at the importance of mindset to success. If you are someone who lets situations get the better of you, or who, despite meticulous planning, never quite performs as well as you'd hope, this stripe is for you. It's time to harness the power of your mind to get the most out of yourself.

Stripe Four:
Champion Mindset

To endure the rigours of sport and life in general, you need to be psychologically tough. It makes sense, given that we all have to deal with setbacks over the years. You will get knocked down and have to pick yourself up. There will be plenty of battles to fight in your quest to reach the pinnacle and it won't be easy. Mentally you need to be up to the challenge: strong willed, thick skinned and resilient. When I was growing up, I was in awe of my sporting heroes such as Steve Redgrave, Kelly Holmes and, of course, Chris Hoy. They were like Greek Gods to me. A level above us mere mortals, they could withstand anything and deliver when it mattered.

It's not all about positivity

It wasn't until I became involved in international sport and began to meet top-level sports people that I realised there was nothing godlike about them. They were normal human beings with the same self-confidence issues that you and I have. If these individuals weren't as thick skinned and resilient as I believed, what was it that separated them from the crowd? How did they overcome self-doubt and perform at such a high level?

I began to realise – and working with my clients has confirmed this – that most successful people have a champion mindset. Essentially, they have a system that allows them to deal with any issues by either setting them to one side or using them to fuel their performance. I was desperate to learn more about this and spent years asking questions and trying things out for myself. This chapter outlines the systems I adopt to achieve the best performance possible. I have shared these tools with people from various industries and the results speak for themselves. What are the components of a champion mindset? What does it take mentally to put in the necessary graft over many years to go from relative mediocrity to number one?

When it comes to personal development, a popular approach is positive thinking. The belief that if you approach everything with a positive attitude, then positive things happen to you. If you believe that you

STRIPE FOUR: CHAMPION MINDSET

will achieve happiness, health and success in your life, then it happens. Although I believe in being positive, I'm not a great fan of this approach. As positive as you want to be, you have to accept that negative thoughts can and will arise. Trying to think only positively often does the opposite and you feel a failure whenever a negative thought pops up. And is every negative thought a bad thing?

There are two key types of negative thoughts. Ones that bring you down and cause a negative outcome. Then there are those that motivate you to become better and create a positive outcome. The key is to recognise which type they are and filter out the first but hang on to the second.

I regularly have negative thoughts, particularly as races approach. As the level of stress ramps up, the lizard part of my brain kicks into overdrive. It's the oldest part and deals with our basic instincts, primarily to do with survival. When your situation calls for a fight or flight response, it's your lizard brain stepping into action. While it's immensely useful when you need it, the lizard brain has an awkward habit of chipping in with things that don't concern it. It believes that every potential new situation is a threat and the best course of action, for your own safety, is to retreat to your normal routine. It tries every trick in the book to convince you that you shouldn't be doing this or that. For instance, if you want to start doing more exercise, it's the part of your brain that comes up with all those reasons why exercise isn't for you. Negative thoughts are its primary weapon and why your mind is flooded with them. This is where I think the positive-thinking approach fails. You can't stop negative thoughts arising. Your best course of action is to observe them and combat them with logic and reason.

I often give time to negative thoughts. By contemplating what might happen if I lose, as well as if I win, I can see there is no reason to be afraid of either outcome. Equally, by thinking logically, I recognise that some negative thoughts are simply an attempt by my brain to sabotage me and I can disregard them. Some athletes prefer not to consider outcomes; they prefer to focus on the process of the race itself. This doesn't work for me. I'm a long-term thinker and so simply thinking through what happens in the race, without considering post-race, feels short-sighted. After all, the reason I am putting myself through this is to reap the rewards of success. Thinking about what could happen if I win is a huge motivator.

By considering all the potential outcomes – positive or negative, I am ready for whatever that outcome brings. It enables me to deal with the situation as it happens. If I lose a race, I know what to do to pick myself up and move on. If I win, then I know what to expect. I remember Chris Hoy telling me that he was so focused on the process of his race at the Athens Olympics in

2004, that when he won gold he had no idea what to do, he'd never considered what would happen the moment after he crossed the finish line. My approach is to imagine what victory might look like. I like to visualise the scene: the roar of the crowd, the standing ovation, the medal. It pushes me to strive for success.

In fact, negative thoughts can be a forceful driver. If you feel as though you have a point to prove or a wrong to right, it can be all the motivation you need. You'll have heard stories about individuals who have overcome adversity, desperate to prove their doubters wrong. The underdog rising up against all the odds to claim victory. Using adversity to fuel improvement can be extremely powerful if used correctly. It's something I've certainly employed during my own sporting career.

One memory comes to mind. I remember talking to my athletics coach when I was about fifteen or sixteen. I'd had little success up till then, but I always tried my best and enjoyed it. I told him the times I'd like to run for the 100m and 200m the following season. He took one look at me and started laughing, 'Well, it's good to dream big.' His reaction made me really angry. I trained incredibly hard that winter. Whenever I found it tough, I'd relive that reaction. I would get angry, the adrenaline flowed and my desire to prove him wrong increased. I pushed myself harder than ever before. On the very first race of the season I nailed those times. I'd harnessed my anger and frustration, using it to get more out of myself. It's also worked in my cycling career. In the run-up to the London 2012 Paralympic Games, British Cycling decided the tandem pairings. I was on the 'B' bike – in other words, second favourites. It felt like a slap in the face; I became focused on proving them wrong. My drive was higher than it had ever been, and I pushed myself every day. As you know, I came home with gold and silver medals.

Perhaps this approach works for me because I have always been self-conscious. I've always felt as though I have had my 'doubters' and this means I tend to work best when I have a point to prove. For some people it leads to a negative performance; they see criticisms or knock-backs as reasons to either walk away or simply accept them. That's never been my attitude. In my opinion, a champion is someone who has to deal with setbacks, but just keeps getting back up. They aren't necessarily mentally tough or robust. The setbacks might hurt, they may take time to get over, but the key is that they turn that negativity into a driver. It spurs them on to put in the time and hard work.

Embrace both your negative and positive thoughts – they occur regardless. Use both as motivation, just adapt your mindset. At the end of the day, you are the one who has to prove to the world what you are capable of. If people think you don't have it in you, envisage what it would be like to prove them wrong.

TAKE ACTION

Pay attention to your negative thoughts.

- When do they occur and are they logical?
- Disregard any thoughts that are clearly an attempt by your brain to sabotage your performance.
- Consider the negative things that have happened in your life; could you use some of them as motivation?

I've often used my visual impairment as a motivator. I love to prove to the world what I am capable of, rather than using it as an excuse to give up. Could you take a similar approach?

CREST your limiting beliefs

Filtering out negative thoughts can work well, but sometimes a specific thought keeps coming back. As much as you try, it persists. If you can't transform it into motivation, you need a way of dealing with it. I have created a system that can be very effective. Before we delve into this, it's important to understand what a thought actually is.

During the course of a day, it is estimated that you have somewhere between 60,000 and 80,000 thoughts. That's a staggering 40 to 55 thoughts per minute. Many will be positive, and many negative, the key is that *none of them are statements of fact.* When you realise this, you can observe your thoughts for what they are, a series of fleeting electrochemical impulses firing in your brain. We all tend to assume that our thoughts are reality, crucially they don't all need to be acted on. Here is an example that happened to me. Let me take you back a few years.

Following on from my success at London 2012, I was honoured to receive an MBE for services to cycling in the New Year's Honours List. On the day of my investiture, I went to Buckingham Palace with my three guests: my fiancée Lora, my mum and my sister. When we got to the palace, they went to the viewing gallery and I was shepherded away to join the other award winners. It was an incredible experience, immensely humbling. I started chatting to a woman who was baffled as to why she was to receive an MBE. When I asked her why she had received it, she said it was for volunteering. She then proceeded to tell me how she had volunteered her time to help others for over fifty years. I pointed out how incredible she was and was probably far more deserving of the award than anyone else.

We were informed that the Queen would be making the awards. As she was performing fewer investitures, we felt immensely privileged. The tension in the room was palpable. The nerves were kicking in. 'What happens when your name is called?', 'How do I address the Queen?', 'How do I know when I have to go up?',

'What happens if I trip up?' These were just some of the questions the staff were being bombarded with.

Before I knew it, it was my turn. I followed some others into the corridor. The queue gradually got smaller as people went to collect their honours. Forget any start lines – this was tension. At least on the tandem I knew what I was doing. Suddenly I heard my name called out and I stepped forward. I received my medal and the Queen asked me about cycling and my plans for the future. Of course, I was perfectly polite though my voice did shake more than normal. But something peculiar was happening. While I was talking to the Queen, I had this ridiculous thought that I couldn't get out of my mind, 'I wonder what would happen if I were to punch the Queen in the face.'

The entire time I spoke to Her Majesty, I imagined being tackled to the ground or shot by a bodyguard. I desperately tried to stop thinking about it, but inevitably when you try to forget something, it always sticks in your head – that old adage of 'when you resist, it persists'.

The point of this story is to demonstrate two things. First, that trying to get rid of a negative thought by trying not to think about it, doesn't work. Second, thoughts are not reality. You can have some ridiculous thoughts, particularly in high-stress situations. This doesn't mean that you need to act upon them. And don't worry, I can assure you I didn't punch the Queen. She is a wonderful lady and I was so honoured to meet her.

If you experience recurring negative thoughts, let's call them limiting beliefs that affect your performance, you need to find a way of dealing with them. I have a simple system that I use in everyday life and when competing.

Imagine your limiting beliefs are mountains that block your way. You can't find a way around them or through them; the only way to conquer them is to *crest* the mountain. I refer to my system as the CREST methodology.

Clarification: The most important step is to clarify that your thought is a limiting belief. I define a limiting belief as a negative thought you regularly have which either prevents you from taking action or brings you down by lowering your self-confidence. Here's an example of one of my own limiting beliefs. When out-and-about, I occasionally bump into things in public. As a visually impaired person, this happens more than I like. My first feeling is embarrassment. I feel incredibly self-conscious and angry with myself. The thought that pops into my head is something like, 'I am an idiot'. It affects my self-confidence for the rest of the day.

I clarify that this is a limiting belief because I think it *every* time I walk into something. It impacts negatively on me and can prevent me from performing at my best.

Once you've clarified this, it's time to move to step two.

Reflection: Reflect on the limiting belief, bring in some objectivity. Look at your situation. Why are you having this thought in the first place? Is there a specific theme to it? Or a specific occasion when this belief occurs? Is it possible it's your lizard brain trying to prevent you from doing something new or different?

When I reflect on my belief that 'I am an idiot', I see that it generally happens when I've walked into something. I realise that it's because of issues I have in accepting my own limitations. When I was growing up, I always tried to hide my disability, obviously this belief still lingers.

Extrospection: When you are in the middle of a situation, it's hard to see the bigger picture. It's time to get a fresh perspective. Rather than focusing on your own point of view, look at it from other people's perspectives. What would someone else say about your limiting belief? Better still, if someone else was in your shoes, what would you say to them?

I have shared my limiting belief with other people. They are always quick to point out that as a visually impaired person, it's perfectly understandable for me to occasionally walk into things. Many fully sighted people do the same. What's their excuse? Then they remind me that probably no one even noticed, and if they did, they will forget it pretty quickly. Certainly, far more quickly than I do.

Substitution: Hopefully, by now you realise that your limiting belief isn't worth heeding. But for this system to work, you have to substitute it for something else. The next time you find yourself in a situation where this belief pops up, you need an alternative belief on standby. It could be something positive or recognition as to why this belief keeps popping up.

My substitution for 'I am an idiot for walking into things' became, 'It's OK, you're visually impaired.' Rather than embarrassment and anger, I can now laugh at it. It means the incident is quickly forgotten and doesn't make me feel bad for the rest of the day.

Take action: The whole point in CRESTing your limiting beliefs is to go out there and be the best you can. Champions don't become champions by sitting around not trying. They find a way to overcome their obstacles, to CREST their mountains. In truth, what have you got to lose? People don't remember those who don't try.

This technique doesn't guarantee instant success – there will be the odd failure. Perhaps you think this means you will be remembered as a failure. Don't worry, you won't. What you will be remembered for is dedicating your life to something and becoming a champion. Stop listening to those negative thoughts and whatever you do, do not under any circumstances punch the Queen in the face!

TAKE ACTION

Work through the CREST method. It's not a complex procedure:

- Take time to examine where and when your limiting beliefs occur so you can reflect on them logically.
- Look at them from different perspectives; you will quickly realise that there are alternative ways of thinking.

Why not challenge yourself to try something that your limiting beliefs have been preventing you from doing.

Mantra

If having drive and a strategy is level one, having the tools to deal with limiting beliefs is the next step. Champions reside at an even higher level. They can shift their mindset when the situation demands. In this section, we explore one of the most commonly used techniques by top sports people, as well as examining a tool that has been integral to my own success.

As I mentioned, you have between 60,000 and 80,000 thoughts per day. This means a constant stream of thoughts running through your head, an internal monologue. No matter what you are doing, your stream of thoughts keeps going. In stressful or challenging situations, it's likely that these thoughts shift from positive to more negative. This is when your limiting beliefs can worm their way in: 'I can't do this', 'This is too hard', 'I'm too tired', 'I don't have enough time'. Even high performers have these thoughts. Imagine what thoughts you might have just as you were about to sink a putt to win the Ryder Cup. Or if you were stepping up to take a penalty in the World Cup Final. The top stars of sport aren't gods or cyborgs, they have similar thought processes to you.

Many sports people, as well as high performers in other industries, use self-talk. It's a way of stopping your brain from simply doing as it pleases. You can shape your thought process to your advantage. Usually self-talk is internalised, however there are times when you can see it in action. You often hear Andy Murray berate himself after a string of bad points. Famously, Maddie Hinch, the goalkeeper from British Hockey's gold medal team in Rio 2016, had notes on her water bottle. I like to repeat phrases to myself before I do something really challenging such as attempting a new personal best weight in the gym.

There are five different forms of self-talk, four of which are useful in different scenarios. Which you choose to use and how you use them is completely up to you.

Negative

The first form of self-talk is negative. We have discussed this previously and it can often take the form of limiting beliefs. It is a monologue that criticises you or the situation you are in. Not only is it not useful, it can often be detrimental. An example of this following a bad performance in training, might be, 'That wasn't good enough. You're obviously not in good shape just now. How are you going to be able to perform in your next session?' And so on.

When negative self-talk takes over, employ the CREST methodology.

Calming

In high-pressure situations it is helpful to reduce your stress levels and heart rate. Calming self-talk is a great way of shifting your train of thought to something that provides a calming influence. It takes a little practice but is easily learned. These thoughts take the form of self-reassurance. In the days leading up to a major race my stress levels increase. The last thing I want is to be on edge for three or four days beforehand. This is the type of self-talk that says, 'You'll be fine, you've been in this situation before. You know what to expect, nothing bad is going to happen. You've done all the hard work, you're in a good place.'

You might find it useful to use calming self-talk before a presentation or an interview. However, I prefer to be fired up for these situations. I find calming self-talk works best for me when I need to be relaxing, but my mind is racing. Sleeping in the run up to a Paralympic Games is notoriously difficult; it might be the same for you the night before a big day. This is an ideal time to use calming self-talk.

Motivational – positive

Positive motivational self-talk is all about telling yourself how good things are, how positive the situation you are in is and how well things are likely to turn out. Widely used in sport, this a great tool to use when times are tough, and things are getting to you. Set your modesty aside in these situations. Remember it's an inner monologue and there is no harm in reminding yourself what your strengths are. If you've had successes in the past, now is the time to mention them. Self-doubt and a negative train of thought can spiral out of control, it's important that you recognise when this is happening and counter it with some positive self-talk.

I like to be fired up for a race. I run strongest on emotion and when it can be harnessed correctly, this is immensely powerful. Motivational self-talk is vital to me in the moments leading up to a race. Both internally and externally I shout at myself. Generic phrases such as 'Come on' and 'You can do this' work well. It's all about working yourself up into a state of readiness for battle. This awakens all the senses, gets the blood flowing and focuses the mind. You are entering into the territory of fight or flight: it's time to fight.

Motivational – negative

A second type of motivational self-talk can be equally effective but takes a slightly different form. This is where you use negative drivers to fire you up to succeed. Do not confuse this with negative self-talk where you talk yourself out of doing something. This is all about inspiring or motivating yourself to act. Some people feed off praise and deliver their best when they feel they are in a positive place. As we discussed earlier, negative factors can also be highly motivational. Most people sit somewhere in between and thrive off both depending on the situation.

When the going gets tough and I struggle with a rigorous training session, I use different types of negative self-talk techniques. First, there is no doubt that extremely tough training hurts. Your body aches and you know that to make it stop you just need to step off the bike or away from the weights machine. That's when I like to address the pain in my body. I'll ask if that's all it's got. I'll tell it, 'If you think that hurts, just wait until you feel this,' before I push myself even harder.

I also think about how hard my competitors are working, I convince myself that they are pushing themselves this hard and if I want to succeed, I need to push harder. When all else fails, I can be heard shouting, 'Come on dickhead'. It might not be clever, but sometimes it's what you need to spur yourself on to the next level.

Instructional

The final type of self-talk takes the form of instructional sayings to remind yourself what you need to do. Let's look closer at Team GB Hockey goalkeeper Maddie Hinch's notes on her water bottle for the 2016 Olympic finals. She had written a few key words or phrases to remind herself of what she needed to do during the match. Written in large capital letters was 'STAY BIG'. This is something all goalkeepers try to remember, to make it harder for the opposition to get the ball past them. It proved vital in that match as Maddie denied the Netherlands from scoring any of their four penalties. Team GB won the gold medal and entered into British sporting history.

Sport is about executing what you have practised again and again during training on the day that it matters. When the pressure is on and the competition is at its most fierce, it's easy to forget everything you've worked on. Having a few simple key phrases to remind yourself what you need to do can be vital to performance. Prior to racing the kilo, I remind myself of a few key things I need to do to ride the perfect race: 'Attack the start', 'Strong, quick turnover' and 'Strong and smooth' are a few examples of them.

The rule of three

Did you notice that most of my phrases have something in common? They consist of three words. I love self-talk that can be delivered in three simple words. There is a theory that our brain works best when dealing with things in threes. For instance, we like a story to have a beginning, a middle and an end. We also find stories that contain three main characters or plot lines most compelling. Medals are awarded to the first three in an event and we tend to remember things in groups of three. Which leads me to believe that our brain works best with phrases made up of three words.

This is particularly relevant with regard to a specific type of self-talk – the mantra. A mantra is a phrase that you repeat internally to bring your focus back to where you want it. If your mantra consists of three words, you will find it powerful. A mantra has been crucial to my own success. Global companies and organisations use the rule of three in their straplines and advertising slogans. For example, can you recall the three words Nike or Audi use for their advertising slogans? For the Olympic Games, it's 'Faster, Higher, Stronger' and for the Paralympics, it's 'Spirit in Motion'.

We have already touched on the All Blacks, the New Zealand rugby team. To become one of, if not the, most successful sporting teams of all time doesn't happen by chance. We saw how having a list of principles that the players live by ensures a seriously strong team ethos. The All Blacks use the power of the three-word mantra on the pitch. In fact, they've taken it one step further and substituted the words with abbreviations. This allows them to be instantly reminded of what they need to do during a match, when split-second decisions can make the difference between winning and losing. A few examples, outlined in James Kerr's *Legacy*, are:

TQB – Top Quality Ball

OTG – Over the Gain Line

KBA – Keep the Ball Alive

LQB – Lightning Quick Ball

I have one favourite mantra that helps me through most tough situations. No, not 'Come on, dickhead', though that might be second favourite. You needn't look past the title of this book, *Earn Your Stripes*. Each year I set out on a rainbow-striped quest to either defend or win the World Championship title. It's why I created the mantra, 'Earn your stripes'. If I am to win those stripes, I'm going to have to earn them. When training gets tough, I know by saying those three words to myself, my focus and motivation snap back into place.

It reminds me why I do what I do and has helped me push myself harder in training than I thought possible.

TAKE ACTION

Before facing a high-stress situation, spend time thinking of useful phrases to say to yourself.

- Try out different types of self-talk. Some situations call for calming talk, while others call for motivational or instructional talk.

- Try to recognise when you fall into a spiral of negative self-talk and switch to another form to break the cycle.

- Think of three-word or three-letter mantras you can repeat to yourself to help motivate you to new levels of performance. Use it whenever self-doubting thoughts creep in.

- Silently repeating your mantra can fire you up and motivate you to chase your goals.

- The more you repeat your mantra in your daily life, the more effective it becomes.

Never underestimate the power of the mind.

Dealing with setbacks

The more you put yourself out there, the more setbacks you have to face. If you're not suffering any setbacks, then I'd probably argue that you're not pushing yourself hard enough. Failures are the only way you are going to improve. Despite this, setbacks can be difficult to deal with. The mark of a champion is someone who gets back up after each setback and pushes themselves to greater things. A champion mindset is being relentless in your dedication to achieving your targets and goals. It's dogged determination to overcome any hurdles in your way. The myth is that you need to be mentally tough to be a success. Mental toughness or resilience isn't about having a thick skin or not caring what others think of you, far from it. I know countless champions, including myself, who suffer self-confidence issues. What champions do have is a system to deal with inevitable setbacks. Knowing they have a system in place ensures they have the confidence to push themselves into situations where failure is an option.

The year 2019 started better than I had planned. All sights were set on the World Championships taking place in March in the Netherlands. With the Tokyo Paralympics just eighteen months away, it was a critical time to lay down a marker both to the rest of the world, but perhaps more importantly, to British Cycling. A blistering performance would ensure the selectors at British Cycling considered me the go-to guy for the Games. My biggest rival was my teammate, James Ball. When you ride for British Cycling, even making the Games is a monumental achievement in itself.

We had two events in January to test where we were in our preparations, as well as an opportunity for the team to score some much-needed qualifying points for Tokyo. The first event was the International Paracycling Cup, taking place on my training track in Manchester. Competing in the place where you train day in day out is always interesting. It can be a challenge to get yourself psyched up in the same way as you would when racing at a completely new venue. This is something I've had to deal with over the years; on race day I was mentally firing on all cylinders.

Although I was competing in two events, the one-kilometre time trial and the sprint, our main focus in recent years had been on the kilo. Unfortunately, the sprint was dropped from the Paralympic programme following the London 2012 Games. This was a tough setback to bounce back from. All funding for Olympic and Paralympic sports in the UK comes from UK Sport. Funding is based on medal success at the Olympics and Paralympics, which means these events take precedence. My funding is therefore now entirely based on my performance in the one-kilometre time trial.

At the time I was riding with Matt Rotherham. Like Pete, Matt came through the Olympic programme Academy system. Things didn't really work out for Matt during his first stint with British Cycling, but time away from racing, and training on his own, helped him develop into a world class rider. He had the opportunity to try out as a tandem pilot and he excelled. Matt is enthusiasm personified. If he sees a challenge, he throws everything at it to succeed. His energy is infectious and great for team morale. I always joke with Matt that I'm the perfect partner for him as I rein in his enthusiasm with a bit of realism. Mind you, I genuinely believe this is why we ride well together.

Race day came and as usual so did the nerves. Despite years of racing, I always get nervous. Nerves are good, nervousness is your body acknowledging and readying itself for the fight. An evening race is always a challenge, the nervous energy buzzing around your system all day can be draining. This time I did an excellent job of killing time. My Christmas present from Lora, a 5,000-piece Lego Tower Bridge, was a fantastic distraction. As this was the first proper race of the season, I had no idea what to expect from my performance. I knew we were going relatively well over a lap, but the one-kilometre time trial is a four-lap race. How would we fare over the full distance? What sort of shape were our teammates in?

I arrived at the velodrome, got set up and began my race warm-up. Negative thoughts kept popping into my head, 'Come on Neil, earn your stripes,' the self-talk kicked into action. I watched as my rivals and teammates clocked solid times, nothing earth shattering, but nonetheless impressive for this stage in the season. It was our turn. As expected, we made a strong start, bursting out of the gate. The first lap felt solid and aggressive, but as the race progressed, I felt I faded pretty badly. Would it be enough for the win? Had we scraped a win in the first race of the season?

Matt turned to me as we crossed the line, 'What's the world record?' he shouted. '59.4, why?', I asked, a little confused. '59.4 what?', he asked. 'I can't remember.' At that moment we heard the announcer say, 'I think that is in fact a new world record!' 'Right, OK, so we are in pretty good shape,' I thought. The world record had stood for five years; Pete Mitchell and I had set it at altitude in Mexico. Riding at altitude makes an enormous difference to times. The air is thinner so the bike travels much quicker. To set this time in Manchester in January was insane. Sadly, as no anti-doping officials were present the time couldn't be ratified. This was very frustrating given the fact I had been tested the day before during a training session. Two days later we followed up with a gold medal in the sprint.

Less than two weeks later we were racing in the National Championships, again in Manchester. Could we get close to 59.422 seconds? Our race day followed much the same pattern as the last time: nerves, Lego, velodrome, warm-up, race. As reigning World Champions, we were last to race, and I had to watch my teammates go before us. They rode an incredible ride, making vast improvements from two weeks earlier, around 1.5 seconds quicker with a time of 59.866 seconds. 'Where did that come from?' I asked myself. It meant they were only the third tandem ever to break the 60-second barrier at sea level. 'What if we don't beat that? Well, it's only the National Championships, it doesn't really matter, right?', reasoned the emotional side of my brain. I've come to realise that in times of physical or mental stress, our brains like to convince us to stop what we're doing and go for the easy option. A classic case of the lizard brain kicking into action. The safe option would be to not fully commit, accept a solid second place and move on with no repercussions. Recognising what my brain was up to, I knew I needed my mantra to snap out of it, 'Come on, Neil, earn your stripes!' This time I shouted it out.

With my lizard brain switched off, I fully committed. Another strong start. We rode well and it felt better than our ride a couple of weeks earlier; but was it quick enough? 59.278 seconds – a new world record. This time it was ratified. In the space of two weeks we had broken the world record twice; a record that had stood for five years. I was most proud of the fact that our time was quicker than any able-bodied solo rider has ever achieved in the one-kilometre time trial at sea level. It means we are the fastest in the world. I feel like this is a real marker to show how far parasport has come. I may not be able to see to ride a bike safely around a velodrome as well as an Olympian, but I can ride as fast as one.

The World Championships were less than seven weeks away. We had to do everything to make sure we maintained the gap over our teammates, as well as our international rivals. Everything was going incredibly well, our performances continued to improve, and we started to mention our desire to become the first bike ever to break the 59-second barrier at sea level.

I changed the name of our team WhatsApp group to Project 58. Matt, our coach Tom Hodgkinson and I were all excited about the challenge.

On 14 February, Valentine's Day, and four weeks before the World Championships, we prepared for one of our hardest training sessions. The stints replicate lactic acid production in the one-kilometre time trial and are excruciatingly painful, but they get results. We knew that after a few weeks of this, the back end of our race could potentially benefit. In the last lap of our first stint, my legs were burning and my breathing shallow and rapid. We came around the last corner and pushed hard for the finish line, desperate to end the pain. Head down, I lunged for the line and then bang. Before I knew what was happening, we were sliding along the track at over 60kph. There had been several near misses in recent weeks. As we slid, I heard Matt say, 'I told you something like this was going to happen,' before shouting in pain. Had they put the starting gate out and we'd hit it? I shouted at Matt to ask if he was OK. When the bike finally came to a stop, I lay on the track still strapped to the pedals. I wondered why nobody had come to find out if I was OK. Twenty seconds or so later a teammate, Mark Stewart, appeared. I couldn't work out why he was the first person to appear and not one of the coaches who'd been standing near the finish line. I was angry and confused. I was panting. My legs ached. Within a minute or two more people arrived and slowly helped me up, asking if I could feel my feet. A legend of track cycling, Kristina Vogel from

Germany, suffered a horrific crash in 2018 that had left her paralysed from the chest down. The incident was still fresh in our minds.

I was helped to the fence on the side of the track. When I looked back there was a group of people about twenty to thirty metres away. Someone was lying on the floor. What had happened? It made no sense; I'd seen Matt get up. He was bleeding and in pain, but he was OK. I was completely disorientated and close to vomiting after all the effort of our ride followed by the crash and hitting my head. Another member of staff ran past, 'Is he out cold?' 'Was who out cold? Had we hit someone?' I was starting to panic.

There was another shout, 'Who is it?'

'It's Dan.'

Dan was one of the paracycling coaches. I was trying to work out all the possible scenarios. 'If we've hit him with the tandem at over 60kph he could be dead. How could this happen?' The world around me might be a blur, but I knew the consequences. 'Dan, stay down, you're OK but I need you to stay where you are.' When I heard that, the relief was immense. He might be hurt, but he's still alive.

I was helped to the medical suite in the National Cycling Centre and sat quietly. I watched as Matt was helped in and lay on his side; it was clear he'd taken a huge hit to the head. Then fellow rider, Jody Cundy, was brought in on a wheelchair. What had happened to him? He was helped onto a bed and said very little. We heard that Dan had been taken away by ambulance; he had dislocated his elbow, broken his shoulder and taken a heavy knock to his head. But he was alive and OK.

It transpired that safety protocols, or lack of them, had broken down. As riders we'd highlighted concerns over the previous months about several near misses; sadly, our luck had run out. Thinking we'd completed our ride, Dan had wheeled Jody on to the track for a handheld start. They were on the track as we came careering round the bend and ploughed straight into them. The aero bars on the front of our bike were like bull horns. Fortunately, we hit Dan slightly to one side, which resulted in the dislocated elbow. A direct hit to the spine would have been catastrophic. Helpless, poor Jody was dragged on the ground by our tandem as we slid along the wooden track. It was a miracle that nobody was more seriously hurt, but our World Championship chances were in tatters.

I suffered skin loss and a slight knock to the head, but nothing major. I tentatively got back in the gym the following day. My body ached but I didn't want to take any time away if I could help it. My right hand was worst affected, but I could still grip reasonably well. I was cleared for concussion and allowed to proceed with caution. Matt wasn't quite so lucky; the knock to the head was far more serious. He spent the next week feeling ill and with no appetite, which is a sure sign something is far from right. Concussion protocol meant he was not allowed to train. It was a tough time, but he was as patient as he could be. Within two weeks of the crash he was cleared to get back to training. Exactly two weeks after the crash, we were back on the tandem. The World Championships were due to take place exactly two weeks later. We would just have to assess our situation.

We met with our coach daily and continually re-evaluated the plan. We analysed our every training effort to see where we were still strong and where we were lacking. We knew time was against us and as such compromises had to be made. The decision was made to focus entirely on getting the bike up to speed and hope that the back end of the race would take care of itself. The first few efforts back on track were steady. While we may have wanted to be back to world record pace, it wasn't realistic; we were a long way off. This was hard to deal with mentally. Less than two weeks away from a World Championships and churning out average performances, while your teammates continue to progress, is a bitter pill to swallow. We kept the faith as best we could and the week leading up to the World Championships saw our form begin to return. Maybe we did have a chance.

TAKE ACTION

You will suffer setbacks. These are the challenging times when it's easy to give up.

- Take stock of where you are, what you can learn from the experience and what you need to do to get back on track. It is, of course, easier said than done.
- When setbacks cloud your judgement and leave you focusing on the negatives, use self-talk.
- Recognise when your lizard brain is pushing you towards the easy way out. Remember what the end goal is and see whether there is another way of getting there.

It may take time to bounce back from setbacks, but you are a champion with a champion mindset. Bounce back, be relentless.

Visualisation

Another tool that is widely used in sport and other fields is visualisation. Although I was never taught it, it was something I practised from a young age when it was probably more akin to daydreaming. If I wasn't playing sport, I'd be imagining myself running, jumping, cycling or scoring incredible goals on the football pitch, wearing either an Aberdeen or Scotland top.

Visualisation can be used in a number of ways and for a variety of reasons. They can range from helping you to relax to firing yourself up to compete on a global stage. Visualisation can help to map out your future or to take part in something that's about to happen. In this section we explore some of these techniques and the situations I use them in.

One reason why visualisation is so powerful, is that it can trick the brain into believing that what you picture is real. This is useful for controlling the part of your brain that can cause problems. Remember that your lizard brain only cares about survival. It reasons that since you are just fine right now, any change is potentially a bad idea, as it might result in death. While you know that advancing a few steps in the world is unlikely to kill you, your lizard brain isn't so sure. What often happens is that you unwittingly self-sabotage when you do take that first step. This is your lizard brain finding a way to draw you back to safety, somewhere it is comfortable. This can be difficult to overcome, but if you visualise yourself performing at a higher level, when you do actually take that step, it won't be such a shock to your lizard brain which will be more inclined to let you continue on your way.

Long-term visualisation

Visualisation for long-term success is commonly used for goal setting and goal getting. Personal development coaches ask you to imagine yourself in your dream job, living your dream life. They ask you to picture this life in as vivid detail as you can, so that you can see it, smell it and taste it. This can be a really useful technique, but with a caveat. I don't buy the old adage that 'If you dream it, you can be it.' I believe that in order to get the most out of this technique you need to add a further step. Visualise your dream life, but from that vantage point, look back and figure out the steps you needed to take to get there. Once you do that, this technique can be immensely powerful.

The best way to do this is to find somewhere that's free from distraction. As you become more experienced and comfortable with visualisation, you will be able to do it wherever you are. Find somewhere quiet and comfortable, preferably somewhere you can sit up straight or lie down if you prefer. Any time of day is fine, though many people find first thing in the morning or last thing at night works well. For best results, close your eyes and shut out any visual distractions. Begin to focus on your breathing, feel your breath entering through your nose. Notice your stomach gently rising with the inbreath. As you exhale, feel the breath travelling up through your body and back out through your nose. Continue to breathe at a rate that you find comfortable, we're not looking for big deep breaths. Keep focusing on your breath as the air travels in and out. If your mind wanders, don't worry, it takes practice. Keep bringing it back to your breath as soon as you notice. It's time to start the visualisation process.

TAKE ACTION

In sport, we work in four-year cycles, so imagine yourself four years from now. I want you to make it as vivid as you can:

- Where are you?
- What does your role involve?
- What are you wearing?
- How do other people react to you?
- What are the sights, sounds and smells around you?

Now, from four years on, look back:

- What did the journey to get there look like?
- What obstacles did you have to overcome to reach that point?

I like to use this technique with major events that are some years down the line. I've spoken about planning four years in advance each Paralympic cycle. These are occasions where I like to think ahead. Many athletes talk about not visualising the outcome, only the process. I don't believe in this. I like to picture myself winning, I want to imagine what it feels like, what it tastes like. I want that image to feel as real as possible because it's what inspires me to want to go and get it. I imagine how fast I've had to ride to win, I think about what I would have had to go through to get there. This process helps to start the planning process and, more importantly, lets my mind, particularly my lizard brain, know that this is something that I want to happen. If it believes that it's in no danger, I can crack on and push myself harder.

Relaxation

The next technique is completely different – visualisation as a means to relax. This isn't something I use very often, but I've explored it now and again. When I struggle to sleep in the days running up to a big race, it can be useful. It's more of a mindfulness exercise, but I find focusing on my breath allows me to shut off the barrage of thoughts. Sometimes this is all I need to help me drift off to sleep.

If you are particularly anxious before an important meeting, or if you struggle with tension and stress, then I recommend trying this. By focusing on your breathing, while imagining yourself in a relaxing, peaceful place, you can drastically reduce your anxiety levels. As touched on before, the reason for this, and this is the key with all types of visualisation, is that your mind can be tricked into believing that what you are imagining is real. The biological responses in your body can be triggered purely by visualising a scenario. It is more evident at the other extreme, when you visualise a situation that makes you excited or nervous. Your heart rate increases, and you start to breathe faster as your body gets ready for action. My heart rate regularly mimics how it is during a race, when all I am doing is lying down and imagining it.

If you have a favourite place, real or imaginary, try picturing yourself there, sitting peacefully, just with your thoughts and no stressful situations to deal with. This process can be combined with a series of muscle flexes and relaxations to help reduce any built-up tension. You can do this by focusing on one part of the body, for instance the shoulders. By tensing the muscles in the shoulders for a short time and then letting them relax, you find that tension will ebb away, leaving you more relaxed and comfortable. Then move to another part of the body. This is another strategy I use in the days leading up to a race.

Performance visualisation

The final technique is using visualisation to ensure you deliver the performance you want, whether it's for that important game-day performance, in your day-to-day activities or, in my case, my training performance.

We all lead busy lives and it can be difficult to remember all the things you need to do to perform at your best. This is where visualisation can help you. I use this technique in the run-up to every race, as well as before many training sessions. I have raced many times in my life, but if you count all the times I've raced in my head, we are talking thousands. By visualising every single detail of my race, over and over again, I can mentally rehearse everything I need to do. It's said that you need to do 10,000 hours in order to master something.[15] Mental rehearsal can actually count towards this. When it comes to race day, I know exactly what I need to do. It has become second nature and no longer requires much mental capacity. It means my focus is concentrated on getting the job done, without having to worry about all the minor details.

The process itself is quite simple and similar to the others. Again, it's best to do it somewhere free from any distractions, although the more experienced you become, you will be able to do it wherever you are. I always visualise the moments before the start of my race, in track centre with all the hype around me. For me it's a race. For you, it could be just before you give a presentation, or before a sales call or any key moment in your life. I often begin my visualisation at the call-up area by the start line. I take myself through the processes I go through pre-race in fine detail.

I sit at the chairs. My helmet is on the floor in front of me with my gloves inside it. I reach down to make sure my laces are tucked away and the buckles on my race shoes are the right tightness. Then I pull the zip on my race skinsuit all the way up. I wipe away any sweat on my palms and slide my left hand into my glove, fastening the Velcro securely, before doing the

---

15   Malcolm Gladwell, *Outliers: The Story of Success* (Penguin, 2009)

same with the right hand. As the race before me starts, I place my race helmet on, fastening the strap and making sure everything is tight and in place. I let out a big breath, nod my head and tell myself I'm ready and I've got this. Our bike is taken to the start line and placed in the starting gate by the mechanics. It's time. Matt, my current pilot, stands up; I do too. We turn and face each other, raise our hands above our heads and high ten, I then slap my thighs, shout 'Come on' and make my way to the start line. Matt gets on to the bike, followed by me. I slip my feet through the straps on the pedals, they are there to keep my feet on the pedals. I reach down to my left, tighten the strap and tuck it away. I then lean to my right and do the same. I take my hands off the handlebars, sit up and look down the track. This is it. I place my hands back on the bars and the official asks if I'm ready. I nod.

The countdown clock next to the track starts ticking, ten seconds, I stand up on the pedals and push my weight back into the ideal position to spring forward when the time comes. All riders take a series of deep breaths in the final five-second countdown; mine is an unusual sequence, but it works for me. Five, I breathe sharply out and then quickly and silently in again. Four, sharply out then in. Three, sharply out, on two I breathe in, one a deep breath in. On zero, I pull hard with my hands on the bars, push my left leg down as hard as I can with a strong straight leg and pull my right leg up as hard as possible. At the dead point, where the pedals are at six and twelve o'clock, I quickly reset, get my hips back and do it again. Strong, steady strokes on the pedals accelerate the bike rapidly round the first quarter of a lap. At this point I transition my weight a little bit further back and focus on a rapid turnover of leg speed. Acceleration is everything here, I can start to move the bike a little more from side to side, ensuring all power travels directly through the pedals. As we reach the start of the bend at the end of the back straight, I sit down and continue to push on the pedals as hard as possible. I must not stop driving for even a split second during that transition. Around this bend it's full commitment, pressing on the pedals as hard as possible. As I hit the home straight, I move my hands forward on the bars, allowing me to tuck down low and get into as aerodynamic a position as possible. I think about producing the highest leg speed possible as we travel around the next bend. Now the bike is reaching top speed, here it's crucial to remain strong, but be smooth as well. From here on in the race is a gradual deceleration. If I fight the bike, then it will slow down quicker. I think about big, round pedal strokes. I think about keeping low and as aerodynamic as possible.

As the race continues the effectiveness of my legs will diminish. My sprint-based energy systems will shut down. It is crucial to hold my form here, everything in my body will urge me to sit up and drink in as much oxygen as I can, but I have to stay in position and pedal strongly. We approach the finish line, I lunge by throwing the bike forward, every split second counts. I realise the outcome, I celebrate, we did it.

I cannot begin to tell you how much my heart rate has increased just writing that down. I can picture that race no matter what situation I am in and it always has the same effect on me. I repeat this process time and time again before a race. It becomes so vivid that my heart rate accelerates as though I am in the race. I have no doubt that this technique has been indispensable to my success. I even use it in training, particularly when I try something new or challenging. Visualising all the things I need to think about during my training effort before I do it always helps. It prepares your body and mind for what it needs to go through. I think it's worthwhile using this technique in everyday life. It will give you the fire and enthusiasm to go out there and smash it. This brings us nicely on to our next and final stripe, performing under pressure.

TAKE ACTION

Experiment with visualisation. I use all three types in different situations. The more you practise, the better and more effective you will find this process.

Long-term

Looking at your long-term strategy, visualise what it feels like to achieve the outcome. Consider how your life might be different, where you might find yourself and the people who are around you. Look back at the journey you would have had to take to get there. By doing this your brain will start to believe this as your future. You will find it easier to overcome your lizard brain and push yourself towards that goal.

Relaxation

If stress is getting to you or you struggle to sleep, use this technique to release tension and switch off your overactive brain. There is a time and a place to be fired up and ready for action, the days leading up to an event are not one of them.

Performance

Repeatedly visualise your performance ahead of a high-pressure situation so that when it comes to delivering, you no longer need to think about the processes involved, they will be second nature. Break it down into fine detail and visualise yourself executing every element and, crucially, see yourself succeeding. I often visualise myself celebrating a victory.

Summary

You've now completed Stripe Four: Champion Mindset. We've looked at how you can use negative incidents as a driver. We've explored how you can overcome limiting beliefs, as well as use self-talk and mantras. We've looked at how to deal with setbacks mentally and finally we've explored different visualisation techniques to boost your daily performance.

The fifth and final stripe looks at how you can use high-stress situations to get even more out of your performance. If you see stress as a negative, this chapter gives you some useful tools to turn challenging moments into performance boosters.

Stripe Five:
Perform Under Pressure

By this stage, if you've mastered the previous four stripes, then you are well on your way to achieving new levels of success. There is, however, one more piece of the puzzle you need to become a true champion. Having a strategy in place and performing at a consistently high level on a day-to-day basis is great, but what happens when the pressure really ratchets up? How you perform under pressure not only dictates how successful you are, but also how people perceive you. As a sportsman, my performance is only seen for a few short moments over the course of my career. It's then that the whole world can watch, analyse and judge. I could be the greatest athlete in the world in the gym or during training, but it would be irrelevant if my performance wasn't up to scratch when it mattered – on race day. In sport we have a word for someone who trains well but can't deliver, a choker. Nothing could hurt more than being known as a choker. And fear of just that is further pressure when it comes to race day. What will people think of me? What will my teammates think of me? What if I make a mistake? My future all rests on this moment.

Preparing for battle

In Olympic and Paralympic sport, everything is geared towards performing on that one day every four years. Many athletes spend their entire careers building towards just one race or event at a Games and it may be the only Games they get selected for. When you look at it that way, you realise just how much rides on that one performance. Funding, future and self-image are all on the line. The world watches; there are thousands of expectant fans in the crowd; TV cameras beam your performance around the globe. The pressure is unbelievable. Some find it too much; nerves and doubt get the better of them and they fall apart; their performance diminishes, and the opportunity passes them by. The effect on the individual can be catastrophic; some never bounce back. On the flip side, the rewards can be astronomical. Potential fame, fortune and admiration await. Their future could be decided in a matter of a few seconds. It's all to play for.

This is an extreme example, but you may face similar moments of pressure in your chosen field. The pressure could be more long-term, not condensed into such a short time frame. However, to progress and become world class, you will find yourself in many high-stress situations where your performance is critical. How do you ensure that your performance doesn't suffer at such times? What if you could use the pressure to your advantage? Is it possible to increase your level of performance when it really matters? This is what marks a true champion, someone who can find a little bit extra to get ahead of the opposition. I pride myself on finding something more on race day. I know that no matter what level I'm at, when the big day comes, I can draw on something extra to turn the situation to my advantage.

Earning this stripe means mastering a few key areas. The first is preparing for battle: you have everything in place and are in the right frame of mind for when the fight kicks off. Of course, things can pop up out of the blue. You can't foresee and plan for every eventuality, but the more you familiarise yourself with the process of getting ready for battle, the easier you will find it to deploy quickly and effectively. My battles are my races and my preparation for these brief encounters is meticulous. It has taken years of strategising, performing and adapting.

I like to focus on the final week leading up to an event. Training changes as you get closer to a race, ensuring you are in the best shape possible. This is known as a taper in the sporting world. The volume of training is gradually edged down, while the quality picks up. In other words, I do less efforts in training, meaning I am less tired. As a result, my fewer efforts get increasingly fast as we get to race day. The ideal scenario is that I peak at the right moment, delivering my best performance on race day.

We've already seen that working smart generally wins over working hard. If your big day is approaching, think about your fatigue levels. If you get to that day having worked yourself into the ground, it's likely that your performance will suffer. Last minute cramming is not the ideal approach. I plan exactly what training efforts I need to do each day, which days I need to take off, and what I do with my time in between. For instance, the last thing I want to do before a big race is be on my feet all day sightseeing. It is essential to plan the final few days in detail, whether you're working towards a product launch, a marketing campaign or presentation. When do you need to put in quality work and when could you be resting to conserve your energy? Quality is the goal. Look for areas where you can make small improvements that add up to a big gain overall. What lifestyle choices could make a difference? Diet, sleep and frame of mind are factors to consider.

When you think about the performance itself, think about any aspects that could be problematic. Ask yourself what the pitfalls might be. Allocate time to either think about them yourself, or, better still, discuss them with your team. Have a plan should something untoward happen. It is extremely rare for everything to go perfectly according to your original plan. It is crucial that you can adapt and react quickly and efficiently under any circumstances.

This was particularly important for me and Pete Mitchell in the 2015 World Championships. We were having issues with our tandem. Every so often on the start, our chain would jump. This caused us to get out of sync, and because the noise sounded like something was breaking on the bike, we'd usually stop to check everything was OK. We had to consider what to do if it jumped on race day. The rule states that you can only get a restart if something has broken. If the chain jumped, we weren't guaranteed a restart. We discussed our plan if the chain jumped during the race and we agreed that we would continue riding and take any lost time on the chin. This discussion proved vital, as sure enough the chain did skip during the start of our race. We avoided any delay that could have arisen by deciding whether or not to proceed, and quickly reset and kept going. We may have lost a couple of tenths of a second, but we still went on to win gold.

Preparing for battle isn't all logistical, you also need to ensure you aren't phased by the occasion. This is where the visualisation techniques from the previous chapter are invaluable. In the week leading up to a big race I visualise the race at least five times a day. Mental rehearsal means I am ready for what is coming, it ensures that I don't default to a state of shock or panic on the big day. I visualise myself executing every aspect to the best of my ability. I see myself both technically and tactically getting it just right. Importantly I see myself winning. The key is to prepare your brain to cope with an unusual situation. Your lizard brain will be less surprised by the situation it finds itself in and its self-sabotaging tendencies will be suppressed.

If, like me, you find that your sleep pattern suffers in the run-up to a big event, don't panic. You'd be surprised at how well you can still perform on reduced sleep for a day or two, assuming everything else is in place. The relaxation visualisation techniques can be enough to shut my thought stream off and allow me to drift off to sleep. Another tactic is to pop my earphones in and listen to something, preferably nothing too taxing. I know a few people who use mindfulness recordings that gently send them to sleep. I've found something else particularly useful. I have an audiobook on my phone that is guaranteed to send me to sleep, not because it bores me, far from it. It's the soothing tone of David Attenborough as he narrates his book *Life on Air: Memoirs of a Broadcaster*.[16] Find out what works best for you and have a go-to plan. Try to make those sleepless hours a thing of the past. If they do happen from time to time it's fine. Accept, adapt and move on.

---

16 David Attenborough, *Life on Air: Memoirs of a Broadcaster* (BBC Books, 2010)

The final element in my preparations for battle is devising a blow-by-blow plan for the day itself. I tend to write this a day or two before race day. It is a timetable of the key things I need to do during the day. I know for a fact that I will be nervous and less likely to make smart choices, or any choices at all, on a race day. I will forget to do things that could affect my performance. Back in 2007, I turned up at the athletics track on race day in São Paolo at the IBSA World Championships without my race kit. As the hotel was over an hour away in the crazy São Paolo traffic, going back for it wasn't an option. I ended up competing in a borrowed vest and my full leg running tights instead of my usual skinsuit. The running tights were for cold days in Aberdeen, rather than the blazing Brazilian sunshine. Needless to say, I've learnt from my mistakes and now I plan things meticulously. If I have my plan saved as a Note on my phone, I can refer to it throughout the day. It means I don't miss anything vital.

The plan is based around fuelling (food), logistics (travel and equipment) and race preparation (the physical things I need to do to be ready to compete). Once I get to the warm-up stage I try not to rely on specific times.

Things often happen on race days that can drastically affect the schedule. Anyone involved in sport knows how wildly inaccurate some schedules turn out. To avoid any problems, don't be too rigid with your own timings. I tend to look at the race schedule and work out at which point in the schedule I need to be doing a specific thing. This ensures I am ready for my race, regardless of what time it actually starts. This is an example of one of my recent race day plans.

08:00	Breakfast	
10:00	Light spin on the bike (20 mins)	
12:00	Lunch	
15:00	Snack	
15:10	Depart for the track – put bike in the van	
16:30	(Heat 11 – Women's 1km TT – Russia)	Begin warm-up
16:50	Into race skinsuit and get numbers fitted	
17:15	(Heat 8 – Men's 1km TT – Sweden)	15 second effort
17:45	(Heat 18 – Germany)	Pre-race effort
17:50	(Heat 20 – Australia)	Head to the start line
18:00	Race	

I don't know how many times having a plan like this has saved me on a race day. When tensions are high, decision-making suffers. Eliminating the need to make on-the-spot decisions reduces errors and stress levels. On race day I just want the day to run as smoothly as possible, with minimal thought. A simple plan like this can be invaluable. Don't rely on your memory in these types of situation, regardless of how good you think it is. Under pressure, all reasonable thought can go out the window. This is something you cannot afford as you prepare for battle.

TAKE ACTION

Identify the key dates in your diary. Plan out the week leading up to the big day.

- Remember that cramming everything in at the last minute leads to increased fatigue and decreased quality in performance.

- Consider elements that could go wrong; how would you deal with them? Simply having a Plan A rarely works in your favour. Be prepared to implement Plans B or C.

- Repeatedly visualise your performance in the days running up to the event. Work through every aspect in your head. The more you see and feel it, the better prepared you will be for the day itself. Shut down your lizard brain before it can derail you.

- Save your detailed plan as a Note on your phone or keep it somewhere you can access it during the day itself.

- Reduce decision-making to a minimum. Refer to the plan regularly, and don't miss anything out.

Pressurised situations cause basic things to slip, be prepared.

Creating ANCHORs

You've done all the preparation; you are ready for battle. The run-up to this moment might have felt like a lifetime or passed in a flash. You might feel ready, you might feel you could have done more, either way, the time has come. Today you go into battle, today is race day. This is your moment, don't let the opportunity slip by.

As there is a lot at stake, nerves will play their part. If you want to be able to perform to the best of your ability when the occasion demands, you have to endure this. I know the horrible feelings: the churning in your stomach, the restlessness, the irritability. I suffer all of these and more. Over the years I've become more comfortable with these feelings. I've accepted that I might need to visit the loo a few more times than my average day; it goes with the territory. I would be concerned if I didn't have this feeling on a day like this. And it's not just racing that affects me, I feel the same before a public speaking engagement, before meeting someone new, even before making certain phone calls. I welcome the nerves; it shows that I value these opportunities, it shows I care.

Before we look at ways to overcome nerves, it's important to get some perspective. Remember that nervousness is essentially the same biological response as excitement, you just choose to frame it differently in your mind. When you are excited, your heart rate quickens, you get butterflies in your stomach and your muscles tense with anticipation. Excitement is a positive feeling that affects your whole body; it is known as psychological arousal.

Whereas excitement is a positive response, anxiety is negative. Can you frame your response differently? Is it possible that the anxiety you feel before your big moment is in fact excitement?

As you get older, it's easier to focus on the potential negative outcomes of a situation, rather than face challenges with the fearlessness of your younger self. When it comes to your big day, remind yourself that this is exactly where you want to be. Putting yourself in this situation was part of the long-term plan; you are on your way to success. I vividly recall walking out of the tunnel into the Bird's Nest stadium in Beijing for my first race at the Paralympic Games. I was completely overawed, but as I walked into the vast stadium, I said out loud, 'I live for this!' In spite of the nerves, I wanted to remind myself, and my lizard brain that was all for me hightailing it back up the tunnel, that this was exactly where I aspired to be.

You have to take charge of this situation, rather than let your nerves take control of you. Frame things in a way that works for you. You are a high achiever and high achievers seize opportunities. Naturally they feel anxiety, they worry about the outcome, but crucially they find a way to push through. Embrace the nerves, take note of how your body reacts and learn from it. You will experience this feeling the more you put yourself out there. These are the moments that bring energy and focus into what you do. They have the potential to bring you some incredible highs, as well as the odd low. I can assure you – the trade-off is worth it. It certainly beats chugging along on the status quo where nothing exciting or different is likely to happen.

Once you've embraced the nerves, the next step is to ensure that you have a way of keeping your focus on the task in hand. If your focus slips, snap it back. Something I use, and which is popular among sports people, is performing a simple action that reminds you of the frame of mind you want to be in.

In Neuro-Linguistic Programming, this is referred to as 'anchoring'. You can link a particular emotion or thought to some form of trigger. It might be something incredibly simple and imperceptible, such as rubbing the tip of a thumb and finger together or making a fist. In sport, it often takes the form of routine or ritual. Who can forget Jonny Wilkinson's pre-kick stance? Hands clasped together in front of his chest; he would stare at the point between the posts where he wanted the ball to go. This was Jonny's anchor. He stood like this countless times, both in training and during matches. He instinctively knew to be calm, to take stock of the situation, to consider all the factors needed to execute the perfect kick. In unbearably high-pressure situations,

Jonny used this trigger to bring him into that moment. Endless rehearsing transformed this pose into his anchor.

These triggers or anchors are not hard to create. It just takes practice; I've created a simple system for you to follow – the ANCHOR method:

Acceptance: The first step is accepting that you are experiencing some form of emotion that's causing a negative impact on your performance. In this example we will use fear. For instance, if you are someone who has to give presentations to a group of colleagues or potential clients, you may experience self-doubt, a dry mouth, shaking and even nausea. These are all symptoms that can affect how you deliver your presentation. Once you have accepted these feelings, recognising that you can shape or change these emotions will allow you to start the process.

New emotion: Decide what emotion you would prefer to feel in this situation in the future. What feeling would you like to swap for abject fear? What emotions would generate your best performance? Let's say you'd like to feel calm, confident and in control.

Call upon a previous scenario: Think back to a situation where you felt calm, confident and in control. It could be a work-based scenario, or it could be from some other part of your life: time spent with family or in a particular place that you find relaxing or calming.

Hold on to that thought: This is where your visualisation skills come into play. Picture that time or place as vividly as you can, focusing particularly on how you felt. Paint a picture in your mind – see it, hear it and taste it. For this to be most effective, feel as though you have been transported there. Spend time noticing the effect this scene has on you and your body and mind.

Overlay a stimulus: Now you need to apply a stimulus that you can use in any situation. Common triggers include touching the tip of your middle finger and thumb together, tapping your toe on the ground or gently snapping an elastic band worn on your wrist. Ideally, you want something that would be almost imperceptible to any onlooker. If you are standing in front of an audience during a presentation, you don't want them to see you performing an overly flamboyant trigger!

Repeat: If you repeat this action often enough, it becomes an anchor. In a highly stressful environment, performing the trigger should instantly shift your mind to your preferred emotion. The action anchors you to your desired emotion. You can perform the trigger before you stand up in front of an audience and several times during the presentation, converting your fear to a feeling of being calm, confident and in control.

In the section on visualisation, I described my routine in the moments before a race. You could say the whole routine is an anchor, but there is one part I deliberately added to act as a trigger. I had been working with a sports psychologist on an issue that I had been struggling with and which was affecting my performance. There had been a phase when things kept breaking on the tandem during starts. This is quite common in tandem racing as it's when the most force is being applied to the bike. The aim is to get the bike from stationary to moving within a split second. It involves two guys (myself and Pete Mitchell at this time) pushing on a huge gear with as much force as possible. This creates an enormous amount of force travelling through the bike at once; in fact, the torque created by two sprinters pushing as hard as they can on the pedals is somewhere in the region of 1,200 newton metres. When you consider that Formula One cars only produce around 700 newton metres of torque, you begin to understand why things might break on a tandem.

Initially, it was just chain jumping, but this started to develop into bigger problems as we got stronger. Sometimes the wheel would pull over or we would strip the sprocket. Wheels had been written off, chains would snap, and we frequently bashed our knees or arms on the bike. Cuts and bruises were bad enough, but worse was to come. We rolled up to the start line to do yet another practice start. Our coach held us upright as we came to a stop on the line. We got ourselves into position and our coach started to count down from five. As he said 'go' we drove forward on the bike with all the force we could, but something weird happened. Before I knew what was happening, I was lying on the track with my coach looking down at me. Pete stood up holding his set of handlebars. The bike had completely sheared in two, our tandem was no more. Fortunately, we were fine: crashing at zero miles per hour wasn't too stressful. What I did find hugely unnerving was seeing a bike that I travel on at around 75kph, completely split in two.

We decided to build more robust tandems, but my fear didn't disappear. I had it constantly in my head that something similar could happen again on the start line. Rather than committing entirely to the start, I began to hold back, as though I wanted to check if there was going to be an issue with the bike. When it comes to racing, this short lapse in effort – regardless how brief – can be costly. Medals are won by a thousandth of a second. It was an issue I had to resolve.

I explained my concerns to my sports psychologist. I described the thought process and feeling of fear. She reminded me that even if the worst happened and the bike did break again, I hadn't really hurt myself. Although I knew this and her reasoning was sound, I still couldn't stop the negative thoughts from popping into my head at every start. Subconsciously, I was sabotaging my own performance. While I appreciated that my brain was trying to save me from physical harm, I needed to know how to overcome it.

This is when we discussed using a trigger. We looked at something I could do on the bike right before I start, something that would snap me back to my training sessions, all those great starts with no fear of breakages or injury. We decided that my trigger was to release and grip the handlebars three times just before every start. The trigger was to remind me to be in the mindset of committing fully to what I was about to do. I practised this in training and rapidly saw a change. I now do it before every race to remind myself to fully commit to the start. This ensures I give my best and minimises the risk of my subconscious kicking in and harming my performance. This gave rise to the ANCHOR methodology that I use myself, as well as teach to my clients. It's a powerful technique that everyone can use in many situations.

TAKE ACTION

In situations where you feel your nerves are getting the better of you, try to change your perspective.

- Excitement produces the same biological response as anxiety, but the outcomes are very different. Try to approach the situation with excitement rather than anxiety.

- How could you employ the ANCHOR methodology in your life?

- Think about situations where your mind gets the better of you and any amount of reasoning with yourself doesn't do the trick. This is an opportunity to create an ANCHOR, a simple gesture that instantly triggers positive emotions. It's time to take control of your performance, even when the nerves kick in.

By taking control, you remain in the moment and can deliver the performance you're capable of.

Using the situation

You've had a run of bad luck, someone's dropped the ball and let you down, something unforeseen has happened. It doesn't matter if you underperform, the reasons for a sub-par outcome are evident and consequently expectations are low. You wouldn't lose face if you didn't come out on top as it's not your fault. Not fully committing to this one would be the obvious option; pick your battles. Does this sound familiar? If so, you've let the emotional part of your brain convince you to take your foot off the gas.

I see these moments as pivotal. I can either choose to listen to my lizard brain and take the easy option or I recognise what's happening and apply the same commitment I would have if everything had gone to plan. When I took the easy option and failed, I soon found out that the sympathy people proffer doesn't make up for the disappointment of underperforming. When I have taken the second option and achieved what I hoped, I got a sense of accomplishment at overcoming the odds.

But what if there is a third option? What if you could use the challenging circumstances to your advantage? What if you could turn a bad situation into a great situation? Bad luck, bad situations and misfortunes create an emotional response. Normally this response is detrimental to your performance. Many coaches and psychologists teach you to block these challenges from your mind. While coping mechanisms are great, they tend to shut off the emotional responses.

If you can harness emotional power in a constructive way, you trump someone who functions on a purely operational level. They say that the highest highs come after the deepest lows. People harness the emotions caused by that low and use them to fuel their performance. I've done this numerous times during my career. Earlier in the book I talked about winning gold at London 2012. This was shortly after defeat at the World Championships and being considered the number two bike for British Cycling. Things had gone against me; I felt aggrieved, as though I'd been treated unfairly. I channelled those feelings of frustration and anger and pushed myself harder than I ever thought possible. The result was incredible.

I also like to use the atmosphere and magnitude of an event to psych myself up. I revel in the occasion; I want to soak it up and put it to use. I choose not to be overwhelmed by it or simply endure it. In the hour prior to a race I go to the track centre and listen to the roar of the crowd. I contemplate what's at stake and work myself into an internal state of controlled aggression. I strut around, I talk to myself, I visualise myself exploding out of the start gate. Before long I'm like a caged lion. I use everything I can to stoke the fire. This might be aggression and determination, but always controlled.

World Championships 2019, it was four weeks since the crash that left Matt and I with concussion (in his case, severe) and abrasions. We had managed to fight our way back to the form we were in prior to the crash. There was a slim chance we might even be in world record shape. If we were going to take gold and the record, I had to give every bit of myself. As we got closer to the start time, I started stoking my internal fire. I used our crash, the changes we had to make to training because of it, the fact our teammates could beat us. This was the World Championships. Everything was at stake.

In the minutes leading up to our ride, breathing heavily I prowled the pit area, 'Come on Neil, earn your stripes, you've got this.' I performed my race visualisations and followed my plan. I made my way to the start line. A high ten with Matt, 'Come on!' I slapped my thighs and walked to the bike which was waiting in the start gate. I got on, strapped myself into my pedals, sat up and looked down the track, 'This is yours,' I said to myself. I felt the handlebars in my hands, ready to commit everything. The countdown clock started: five, four, three, two, one.

A fantastic start, full commitment. I adjusted my position and continued to pedal. We accelerated through the first lap as planned and drove hard into turn one on the second lap. As we entered the corner, the rear tyre made a horrific sound – not the screeching of a tyre on a car travelling too fast around a corner, more like a tyre that was coming away from the wheel. The bike shot up the track and I instantly backed off the power. 'We're going to hit the deck again,' I thought. But we were still upright. Matt wrestled with the bike, trying to pull us back down the track. We heard the same awful noise as we dropped down and shot straight back up the track. Convinced we were OK and the tyre was still on, we pressed on as best we could, despite losing significant speed. We completed the ride and were hit by disappointment.

We couldn't explain what had happened, but it had wrecked our performance. Our teammates rode next and infuriatingly beat us by one tenth of a second. We had to settle for silver. It was a painful moment. I walked around, hands on head, trying to compute the situation. I congratulated my teammates for their achievement, but inside I was furious. I felt robbed. Back at the hotel, we brooded for a while, but I knew we had the sprint the following day. I talked it over with Matt and we did everything we needed to ensure the best recovery possible for sprint day. We planned to show the world what we were capable of. We were going to use this disappointment to fuel our fire.

I woke up the following day more determined than I had ever been. It was time to right the wrongs and take what was rightfully ours – a World Championship title. Sure enough, we were fastest to qualify; our teammates were second. We progressed through the quarter finals relatively comfortably; we faced the Dutch bike in the semis. We had raced them many times over the years. It was a tough battle, but it was clear we wanted it. Our teammates also made it through to the finals, beating a strong Polish team. It was to be an all GB final. I was where I wanted to be; now it was time to take what I felt was rightfully ours.

The sprint is a best of three rides. The first race was led out by our teammates in the opening laps. With just over two laps to go, we attacked with a ferocity that had been growing inside me since the evening before. Nothing on earth was going to stop us going past them. We took the first match. We just had to take the next ride and the title, medal and rainbow stripes would be ours. I knew we had victory in our grasp. We were clearly stronger, faster and hungrier. I wanted to destroy them, to cross the finish line and lift my arms to the sky. Victory would be sweet.

The race panned out much the same way as the first ride. We led out, but a cunning move by Matt ensured that our teammates were at the front again. It meant we were in a fantastic position to attack and we were confident we could go past them. When it came, our attack was decisive; the acceleration was too much for our rivals. The bike felt stronger than anything I'd experienced. My controlled aggression was channelled into the pedals, propelling the bike as fast as humanly possible.

We rode past our teammates and pulled away, creating a 20-metre lead as we went into the final turn. Without warning our front wheel suddenly slipped from under us; we were sliding along the track at over 70kph. I vividly recall hearing the announcer say, 'And the new World Champions...' Silence. We slid up the banking and I braced myself for the impact from our rivals' bike. I knew I would be first to be hit. Fortunately, they swerved up the banking and squeezed through the gap between our tandem and the fence at the top of the track. We continued to slide back down and along the bottom of the track until we finally came to a stop. My head bumped along the ground: fortunately, my helmet did its job.

I was aware of people rushing towards us. Matt unstrapped himself from the pedals and got up. As I couldn't reach my pedals I just lay and waited. After the usual precautionary checks, I was helped to my feet. I walked back towards our pit area, sporting some large holes in my skinsuit and skin. Adrenaline was pumping so hard that I didn't feel a thing. The medical staff wanted me to sit down, but I couldn't stop pacing. 'These bloody World Champs. Right come on, let's just go and do it all again.' I heard Pete and James, our rivals, discussing whether to hand us the victory in the decider. I kept out of it, I was ready to go again, as was Matt. We knew it would take more than skin loss to keep that title from us.

There was an announcement over the PA system. The race officials had awarded the win to us; we were to be crowned World Champions. A quick check of the rule book revealed a regulation we were unaware of. If someone is ahead with an unassailable lead and they crash, then the officials can award them the victory. As far as I know, we may be the first World Champions who didn't cross the finish line.

As soon as I heard the announcement, the adrenaline drained away and the pain hit. What followed was the least comfortable podium I have ever stood on. My track burns ached, and my hand didn't feel right. The worst part was the struggle to put on the striped jersey. Once on, I felt as much pride as I did pain. The fact that the jersey got blood on it and I've never washed it, probably makes it my most prized jersey.

I am a huge fan of using a situation to my advantage. It's why I've developed into someone who performs better on race day than in training. I appreciate that not every situation is the same as being in a sporting arena on race day, but you can adapt this approach to your own circumstances. High performers deliver day in day out, but they pull something special out of the bag on those occasions that really matter. The last thing you want to be is one of those people who's known for performing well in training, but not doing the business on game day. Using this approach, together with everything else we have learnt, will ensure you aren't a choker. Remember to use the emotional part of your brain to your advantage, prepare yourself for action and feel the energy and adrenaline flowing through you. Embrace the nerves, enjoy the experience and live life for the highs. You're well on your way to earning your fifth and final stripe.

TAKE ACTION

See challenges as an opportunity to stand out from the crowd. If you can deliver on those big occasions when it isn't expected of you, you will get noticed.

- Embrace the stress and hype at events that really matter. If you've prepared correctly, then you can trust yourself to do the right thing.
- Use the emotional part of your brain to produce something extra.
- Motivational self-talk, visualisation and mantra will pay dividends.

Go earn your stripes.

Moving goalposts

You've planned well and are making real headway. You have the right mindset and a good team around you. Be careful that your long-term planning isn't like building a skyscraper in an earthquake zone. Too much rigidity will cause cracks to develop and it may eventually come tumbling down. The world around you is constantly changing. Along with the everyday firefighting, you have to deal with new challenges, competitors and various other distractions. If your plan doesn't evolve with you, then you may be in danger of missing out further down the line.

Elite athletes tend to be adaptable. They face the constant risk of injury during their sporting careers. When this happens, they don't just sit back and wait to recover, top athletes find alternative ways to train. They strengthen the areas around the injury, as well as focusing on areas which they don't usually have time for. The result is that the athlete often returns to full training and competition stronger than before the injury.

I am blessed with a degenerative eye condition. This might sound like a ludicrous statement, but it means that I have had to learn to adapt how I approach different tasks. At school I could see the slides in a presentation if I sat at the front of the class. These days I can either take a photo of the slide and zoom in or get the slides in advance on my phone or tablet. It's best if I'm not too precious about how I do things, as I will probably have to adapt it in future. This principle applies to all aspects of my life.

Religiously following plans and failing to adapt rarely ends well in sport, business or life in general. It is essential to review your long-term plans regularly. I encourage my clients to think about what's working, what needs tweaking and what has to go. Hanging on to ideas for emotional reasons is not conducive to high performance. I revisit my long-term goal setting process at least once a year. You should re-evaluate short-term plans at least every couple of weeks. Adaptability is key to your long-term success. Be aware of what your competitors are doing. In both sport and business, someone new will come along and disrupt.

It's also important to accept that people are only human. A support network is crucial, but you can't rely on individuals being there for you indefinitely. Things change and it's essential that you are robust enough to deal with any losses, and adaptable enough to work with new people and in new situations. I've worked with many coaches over the years, as well as support staff and tandem pilots. Change can be intimidating, but I've always found that working with new people has helped me develop as a person and an athlete. It's given me more insight into the world I work in, as well as a better understanding of how I function.

After our interesting World Championships in 2019, the focus turned to 2020. The year began with the World Championships in Milton, Canada, followed by the big one – the Tokyo Paralympic Games. In summer 2019, after much discussion, James and I were swapping pilots. It would give Pete and James the opportunity to try for the number one bike. We would find out how the new pairings faired at an event in November 2019. After that, the selection panel could decide the pairings for Canada and Tokyo.

I was disappointed to break up my partnership with Matt. The previous eighteen months had brought incredible success. Medals, world records and a shared sense of experience from our two crashes. We were a formidable force and I was worried that changing things might upset our chances of future success. Fortunately, riding with Pete was an equally strong alternative. We'd already won six World Championships and get on really well. I knew getting back on track with him could be very successful, but could we edge out Matt and James? A summer of hard training meant the four of us were in great shape. We all wanted to prove what we were capable of.

On 2 September, I received a phone call from Pete's wife Naomi. She sounded frantic. Pete had been in a crash. She had spoken to him and he'd said he was OK, but she was rushing to see him. I assumed it had been a bike crash and though I was obviously concerned, I didn't think too much of it. Crashes are common and usually mean a week or two off the bike. And if Pete had spoken to Naomi then he was probably fine. Later that day I found out that he'd been in a car crash on his way to the velodrome. Travelling at around 70mph on a dual carriageway, a car had pulled out in front of him and Pete had clipped the car, causing him to roll at least three times. Although the roof caved in and the car was a write off, Pete had escaped with whiplash and concussion.

We see concussion regularly in cycling. It generally lasts between a couple of days and a couple of weeks and we assumed that Pete would be fine before too long. I'd just have to train on my own on static bikes; something I had often done over the years. I set my goals accordingly to make sure I was in the best shape possible for Pete's return. Two weeks passed; Pete was still suffering the same symptoms and had made no progress. Concussion protocol meant that he couldn't undertake anything physical until his head felt clear. He was still suffering from dizzy spells and found it hard to concentrate. Knowing that once he did return to training it would take another week before he would be cleared to return to tandem riding, we were on a one-week rolling plan. On a day-by-day basis my time on the static bike would extend. Although I was frustrated, Pete's health was my main concern. I desperately wanted to be back on the tandem, but I had to be patient. I continued challenging myself in training, hitting new personal bests in the gym and on the bike. I was ready to go.

As each week went by, I grew increasingly concerned. The race in late November was fast approaching and I hadn't been in the velodrome for some time. Something needed to be done. I decided to arrange a meeting with everybody concerned to see whether we should bring in a temporary replacement. It would allow me to race and take the pressure off Pete; allowing him to focus on his recovery. We agreed that it was the right option but would probably take time. Finding someone of the calibre and experience of Pete was out of the question. But was there a rider out there who could step up to the task? Another two weeks went by, and I was still training on my own.

I was becoming increasingly frustrated and I used that emotion in my training sessions. The easy option would have been to take my foot off the gas, instead I wanted to prove what I was capable of. I was in incredible shape, lifting personal bests in the gym and outputting my best powers on the bike. I was using my short-term goals to make the most of the time I had. Time was ticking by, however, and I was lacking in tandem time and race craft. The news I was waiting for finally came through. A young academy rider was in danger of dropping out of the British Cycling programme. Rather than switch to a six-month 'last chance' review process, he'd been offered the opportunity to pilot the tandem. This would give him more time on the British Cycling programme to improve. Lewis Stewart is a fellow Scot, a young talent with plenty of strength and quality and I was excited at the prospect of working with him.

There was less than four weeks until the race. Lewis turned to me and said, 'I don't know if I'll be any good.

I've never ridden a tandem before. Just tell me what I'm doing wrong.' It was our first track session. At this stage every session would count. We had to build a relationship and I had to develop trust in his bike handling skills. It would take time to develop synchronicity between us: time was something we didn't have. Day one was straight in at the deep end. Rather than getting to know each other, we went for full commitment. Tricky, technical efforts at high speed that would push Lewis hard. The quickest way to learn is often by going in at the deep end.

We accelerated out of the saddle and the bike jerked violently from side to side. I hung on for dear life and prayed we'd make it to the other end. Afterwards Lewis turned and asked, 'Was that okay? It felt pretty weird.' I was frank with him – there were technical things that he had to change straight away. Despite my better judgement, we got back on the bike and tried again. Remarkably he'd taken it all on board. The bike went in a straight line; things didn't look too bad.

I continued offering advice and Lewis took it in. By the end of our first training session we were clocking times that would be fairly competitive on the international scene. The guy definitely had what it takes. With time against us, we still had a long way to go. Each session was a case of trying something new, ticking the box and moving on to the next. Rapid, quick-fire adaptability. Every day we set new goals, knocked them down and moved on. I wondered how much Lewis could take in and how much would stick under the pressure of race day.

Despite being so new to tandem riding, Lewis seemed confident and calm on race day. He wasn't fazed by the occasion or the situation, he listened to advice and gave it everything. Not only did Lewis deliver, but he rose above and beyond what was expected. Together we finished second in the kilo in a world class time. Only Matt and James had beaten us, there was no shame in that. Having completed the event that counts for the Paralympics, it was time to have some fun. In the sprint we learned lots about each other on the day, continually adapting our plans as we progressed through the rounds. In the final, we came up against our teammates Matt and James. They had qualified much quicker than us and looked to be a little too fast. The performance gap showed in the first ride as they took the win in the best of three gold medal ride-off. An incredibly close second ride followed that Lewis and I managed to nick on the line, before winning the final and taking the gold medal.

Lewis had earned his place on the team and would be heading to the World Championships in Canada. He wouldn't be riding with me though. The decision was made to switch the pairings back. I would ride with Matt, and Lewis and James would form a new partnership. Back riding with Matt I headed to the championships in great form. The goal was to win back the title we'd lost the previous year and to qualify for the Tokyo 2020 Paralympic Games. Victory in Canada in the kilo would essentially book our seat on the plane. On 1 February 2020 we did just that – won gold, won back our striped jerseys and reserved our plane tickets. My fourteenth world title came in another sub 60-second clocking and essentially guaranteed Tokyo selection. Now just one race stands between me and Paralympic gold. The goalposts are always changing, but crucially the end goal is always the same: winning back my Paralympic title.

TAKE ACTION

Revisit your strategy regularly.

- Take note of any change on the horizon, either for your competitors or in your own situation.
- Adapt accordingly, never get too hung up on the original plan. Always have the end goal in sight.
- If things take a drastic turn, explore all the options. Set short-term goals that allow you to make the most of the situation you find yourself in.

Remember, don't be afraid to put your faith in someone or something new.

Congratulations! You've earned all five stripes and made it to the top. It feels pretty amazing, right? One small problem – tomorrow is another day. They say that getting to the top is hard but staying there is the real challenge. There is, of course, some truth in this. You can invest absolutely everything you have physically, mentally and perhaps even financially, to reach the top of your game. Perhaps you are performing at your absolute best and taking the world by storm but be careful of burnout.

Long-term success

Burnout is a state of emotional, physical and mental exhaustion that can follow a prolonged period of stress. If you do suffer from burnout, it can take a while to recover. It often requires you changing something. The problem is the rest of the world won't wait for you to get back to your A game. All that hard work, dedication and time could be for nothing – other than a brief spell in the spotlight.

Burnout is common in sport; athletes who focus everything on their sport tend to be susceptible. Their every action and decision are made solely with their future success in mind, while they push themselves harder and harder in training. Not that this is a bad thing or something to be ashamed of, it just shows how strong the desire is. Focused on going faster and faster, they often overlook the brick wall in front of them. For a long time, people thought this was the right approach – maximum commitment, complete dedication. Now we often hear stories of overtraining and mental problems. And there are those who showed huge potential and then disappeared off the radar. I was very aware of this when I was growing up. I saw athletes with huge potential and who were destined to win it all. Despite being the best in the country, they lost interest and walked away. At the elite level there are countless athletes who have an incredible performance one year, but illness and injury mean they are out of the picture the following year.

The first time I experienced this type of issue was immediately after winning double gold in the 2009 World Championships. I had worked so hard and so long and suddenly I'd achieved great success. The following year I struggled with motivation. I was asking myself, 'Now what?' It took losing my world ranking to make me realise that I needed to make some changes. I can now look back at this stage of my career with pride. I've been at the top for a decade now. In that time things have progressed immeasurably. The world keeps getting better, stronger and faster: but I keep managing to stay one step ahead. The 2009 World Championship was won in a time of 62.2 seconds – 10 years later I was 3 seconds faster.

What has kept me motivated to keep pushing forward? How did I avoid physical and mental exhaustion over the years? Firstly, lifestyle plays a huge role and meeting Lora was the greatest thing for me in that respect. She helped me identify areas where I was falling drastically short. Lack of sleep, poor diet, under hydration and an addiction to computer games were leading me to potential burnout.

I see this again and again, particularly in business. People eat a poor-quality diet, work long hours, saying things like, 'Sleep is for the weak', 'If I can just get this task done, then I will take a rest' and 'I don't have time for lunch.' Inadequate sleep and not eating properly doesn't always mean a lack of performance in the short-term. But the wheels can fall off very quickly. It's certainly not a good way to thrive. Ask yourself whether you want short-term success or to build a legacy? Neglecting your health because you don't have time for it isn't an option. By investing in your health and wellbeing now, you will see the benefits in the years to come.

Finding alternative outlets was crucial for me. For years I had been focused entirely on my sporting career. This is great when things go well, your identity is built around your success and when the going's good you are on top of the world. Inevitably though, there will be tough times, stressful times and days when you feel like packing it in. This is when you need to have another focus. This could be a hobby, time with family or a project. I've had plenty of dark days in my sporting career. Sometimes I couldn't see a way out. My mental health suffered and affected my performance.

There was a phase in my athletics career when I was underperforming. I became incredibly self-conscious about everything I did in training. I felt as though everyone was judging me, analysing me, looking for the tiniest flaws. I imagined everybody was looking at these flaws. It reached a point where I didn't want to leave the house. I was happy to stay in my own room, wrapped up in the world of computer games. I still had enough drive to go to training, but I was very quiet and reserved. During a gym session I had a bit of a meltdown.

It was 2007, the training session was for talented local athletes from different sports in the Aberdeen area. It was a fantastic environment, filled with like-minded athletes coached by people such as Donald Pirie. My first exercise was squats. I did a few warm-ups and loaded the bar. It looked a tough session on paper, but I was more than capable. As expected, the first set was challenging. Then my mind started to play its old tricks. Why was I finding it difficult? Was I doing it wrong? Maybe I just wasn't good enough and I was going to be found out. In between sets I kept my head down. I looked around the room to see where my coach was. He was busy with another athlete. Perfect. I quickly went to do my next set of lifts, desperately hoping he wouldn't notice. I didn't want anyone to see, especially a coach. They would spot immediately if I wasn't good enough or not doing it right.

I completed my set of the squats, completely unseen. Next was bench press. Someone else was using the bench. Rather than ask how long they'd be, or if I could use it between sets, I sat in the corner. When Donald came over and asked how I was getting on, I told him that my squats had been fine, but that I wasn't feeling too well. I didn't have any energy and just didn't feel right. Donald quizzed me about my other sessions and what I had eaten. He helped me set up the bar for bench press. 'I'll spot you,' he said. 'Damn it, he's going to see me,' I thought. I had eight reps to complete, it was a heavy weight, but I was lifting it fine. I could feel Donald watching me. As I got to the end fatigue crept in. Donald helped me put the bar back on the rack. 'Great, you might not be feeling right, but you are lifting the weight fine,' he said. 'No, I just feel really shaky, I think I need to stop,' I replied. There was some discussion, but I decided to leave the session. I had to get out of there, I couldn't stand another minute. I felt as though the walls were closing in and that everyone was staring and judging me.

I escaped to home, safety and comfort, but I felt awful. I knew exactly what I'd done, and I was ashamed of myself for giving in – that wasn't me. I've always been proud of my grit and determination. Who was this guy who had just walked away? I'd love to say that it was a pivotal moment in my mental health, but it wasn't the case. I had no intention of opening up about how I felt. The next time I saw my athletics coach he mentioned that he'd spoken to Donald and asked what was wrong. I think he knew something was not right. His role as a minister probably meant that he knew the signs.

Although we did talk a little about it in the following months, I found it incredibly hard to open up. This low feeling followed me into early 2008, when I was on a month-long training camp in South Africa. It was far too long to be cooped up in a hotel where sport was the sole focus. The first two weeks were fine as the majority of the British Athletics team, both Olympic and Paralympic were out and there was a lot going on. Only a few of us were there for the final two weeks. That's when I started to slip into a 'I don't want to be here' mentality. It meant I failed to get anywhere near the best out of myself. I was burning out mentally and I was losing the drive and determination. I was so involved in my sport that the smallest setback felt earth shattering. I had no perspective.

In the past few years I have spent time building up a business alongside my sporting career. In the early days, I worried that spending so much time on something other than sport could harm my performance. At the time, it was also the mindset of UK Sport. Fortunately, there has been a significant shift in recent years. Now it's recognised that athletes perform better when they have another interest or focus away from sport. The mental break from sport gives them a more balanced perspective and brings a freshness to their training. I find that my performance has dramatically improved since I started spending quality time away. It sounds counterintuitive, but I would encourage you to find another interest. A release from your day-to-day stresses. In the short-term, a few hours away means less gets done, but you will be surprised by how quickly the deficit is both made up and then surpassed. What's more, it means you are more likely to achieve long-term success. I don't want to create super performers who explode on to the scene, only to fizzle out a year or two later. I want to create legacy makers who have the potential to change the world in the coming decades. It's time to get your lifestyle sorted, find an outlet and start building a legacy.

TAKE ACTION

It's important to play the long game.

- Look after your physical and mental health to ensure you perform year on year.
- Plan your day so that you factor in eating, sleeping and exercise so that you approach any activity with a freshness and ferocity that allows you to get more out of it in significantly less time.
- Find an outlet outside of your work to keep things in perspective.
- Think long-term, think legacy.

Having a balanced view on life keeps things in perspective and allows you to thrive in high-pressure situations.

Summary

Congratulations on completing the fifth and final stripe, 'Performing Under Pressure'. Head to earn-your-stripes .co.uk and take the Earn Your Stripes quiz to find out how you score in each of the five stripes and how to make any necessary improvements.

We've looked at how you can use high-pressure situations to get more out of your performance. Plan for key moments using the skills you've learnt in the previous four stripes. Now that you have all the tools at your disposal, it's time to put them into action.

The Comeback

The end?

Rio 2016 Paralympic Games: I have just crossed the finishing line. It has dawned on me that I haven't won gold. This is the moment when my world began to collapse. My immediate thoughts were, 'You've let yourself down, you've let your family down, you've let your whole nation down.' I was devastated. I didn't have time to dwell. Ten minutes after the most painful defeat of my sporting career, Lora was racing for gold in the 3km pursuit. My legs had completely packed in, but I managed to stagger to my feet and stumble towards somewhere I could watch. Lora started her quest for gold; I knew how much this meant to her. She had been destined for gold at London 2012, but a problem with her chain condemned her to seventh place. It had almost destroyed her, but she'd fought back, and this was her moment. You should have heard me roar when she crossed the line ahead of the reigning world champions, New Zealand. She was a Paralympic champion and I was elated for her.

After my medal ceremony, an experience I don't remember with much fondness, Pete and I headed to Channel 4 studios with other members of the cycling team. We were to appear in the audience for the live show, *The Last Leg*. It first aired at the London 2012 Paralympics and has revolutionised how the public view disability. I was asked if I was willing to be mic'd up. Adam Hills the presenter would mention our performance and cut to me for my thoughts. I agreed. The mood was jovial, but I sat in the audience feeling dire. I didn't want to be there; I felt the same as I had in that Aberdeen gym all those years earlier. Just before the first advert break, Adam mentioned a 'fantastic silver medal for Neil Fachie and Pete Mitchell'. The camera cut to me and rather than say anything, I just nodded my head and tried to look pleased. I felt like a fraud, I didn't deserve to be in that studio, the eyes of the nation that I'd just let down were all on me, judging me. I felt sick.

After the show I caught up with Lora and our families. While I was delighted to talk about Lora, I couldn't bear anyone talking about my race and changed the subject immediately. The following few days were tough. We were staying in the athletes' village, and I was surrounded by Paralympic fever. People kept coming up to me to congratulate me on my performance or ask me how I'd done. My reply was, 'Silver medal, second in the world, amazing.' I'm not sure if I was trying to convince them or myself: inside I felt numb. Lora tried to broach the subject as she knew I was hurting. I assured her that I was happy with silver, I was fine.

The journey home felt like a kick in the teeth. The British Airways flight from Rio to London was chartered solely for the team. Multiple gold medallists flew first class, gold medallists and multi-medallists in business class, and the rest of us in economy. While Lora travelled in luxury, I brooded in the back. I was hurting. Everyone was getting drunk, either celebrating or perhaps drowning their sorrows. I had a few, but I just wanted to get off that plane, not ideal at 30,000 feet.

There was a parade through Manchester, an event at Trafalgar Square and a reception at Buckingham Palace. I was delighted to see Lora getting the plaudits she deserved. It was a pleasure to speak to the Queen again. I didn't even think about punching her in the face this time. Just to be clear – I love the Queen.

The following six weeks were crazy, Lora and I had wedding plans to finalise. A post-Paralympics wedding had been in our diaries for a few years. Having it then meant we would both be able to enjoy the day, as well as our honeymoon, without any guilt about missing training or not eating healthy food. It was certainly a non-stop and fantastic distraction, particularly the dancing lessons for our first dance. And when the day came, I can genuinely say it was the happiest day of my life.

When we got home from our honeymoon in South Africa, things started to change. I no longer had distractions other than a return to training at some point.

For the next few months, I wasn't much fun to live with. My poor wife had to put up with me – goodness knows what she thought she'd signed up for. I was finding it hard to compute what had happened in Rio. We should have won, and I was frustrated and angry with myself. I became irritable. Towards the end of the year I was planning to get back to training, when the governing body of cycling, the UCI, did something unusual. There had never been a Track World Championships the winter after a Paralympic Games. At the end of 2016 the UCI decided, with just seven weeks' notice, that there would be a World Championships in Los Angeles in early 2017. Unfit and out of shape, there was no way I could be anywhere near my best in that short space of time, but I knew I had to go for it.

I started training, skipping all the base work that I normally do. I needed to be as race ready as possible. I worked as hard as I could, but admitted it was a losing battle. We turned up in Los Angeles and weren't too surprised to find out that many of the other nations had decided not to attend. It was simply too short notice and most teams had blown their annual budget on the Rio Paralympics. As the Dutch team weren't there, the reigning Paralympic Champions wouldn't be racing, it was a mediocre field.

It was an unhappy camp for me that week. My lack of confidence because of my poor physical shape, as well as the fact I was still trying to come to terms with Rio, meant that I spent most of my time in my bedroom, with occasional trips to the coffee shop with Lora. Race day came and I managed to take a silver medal. The time wasn't too bad all things considered, but the real disappointment came from the fact my teammates won gold. Don't get me wrong, it's great to have a GB one-two, but it was a bitter blow to my overall standing in the team. The following day it was silver again, this time in the sprint, our teammates again taking gold. I went home from those championships feeling dejected.

During the last few days in Los Angeles, cooped up in my hotel room, I began looking at online courses. I wanted to start planning for the future. I felt that I might be coming to the end of my sporting career and the panic of not having a plan was starting to kick in. I'd been a full-time athlete for over a decade and I felt as though I had nothing else to offer the world. The truth was, outside of sport I had nothing, I had no other source of income and, frankly, no idea who I was. After much deliberation, I settled on a Life Coaching distance learning course. I'd not thought about returning to study, but I could see the benefit of having another focus in my life.

The final straw was when I got back to Manchester. We were asked to do some testing on our bikes, just to gauge our base levels of fitness ahead of summer training. I still wasn't in great shape and I dreaded it. My old fears of being seen as a fraud were beginning to surface. Testing meant the data would be there for all to see. I went to the velodrome by tram, I felt like a broken man on his way to be culled. We were told which tests we would do, a few peak power tests on the bike, as well as a couple of more endurance-based efforts. I felt dreadful on the bike; the results wouldn't be back that day, but I knew they wouldn't be great. While my teammates were bubbly and chatty, I didn't say much, avoiding any conversation. I really felt that I didn't deserve to be there.

The last test was a one-minute effort, similar to racing the one-kilometre time trial. This is the test that you know is going to hurt. Despite feeling low, I committed everything I could. As expected, the first 30 seconds were fine, but then came the inevitable fading. The energy systems start to shut off and you feel that you can't push anymore. The lactic acid builds and you must keep going as best you can. The voice in my head was telling me I was pathetic in those last 15 seconds, but I got there. The minute was up. Then the rush of lactic acid hits you like a steam train; it hit me hard. I immediately felt sick. I just made it to the toilet before throwing up my breakfast. This sometimes happens in training. As a young athlete, I used to suffer every session, but over the years my body has learned to adapt. Not today – today was a bad day.

We still weren't done for the day, we needed to have our body fat measured. Another unglamorous part of sport is having your fat measured regularly to ensure you are lean enough for the job at hand. It usually involves someone grabbing your skin and measuring the fat with a set of callipers. This is done in several points around the body. You stand there in your under-wear while someone literally grabs your fat. If you are self-conscious or aren't in the best shape, it's a pretty grim experience. Not only would we have to endure that, we were also having a body scan. This would measure our body fat percentage. I was worried. I stood there miserably as my fat was squeezed; I just wanted the floor to swallow me up. 'Well, I see you've been enjoying yourself a bit.' The readings were by far the highest I'd ever had, and it was clear I hadn't lost any of the post Rio/wedding/honeymoon fat.

Next was the body scan. I took the results to the phys-iologist and waited for the inevitable. 'OK, Neil, your current body fat percentage is 19%. We could probably do with that coming down a little bit.' 'So, is that OK for a sprinter, do you think, maybe just a few percent high?' I asked. 'Honestly, it's pretty high. A lot of the guys are under 10%, looks like you have a bit of work to do.' It was then that I started to notice that some of the support staff had doubts as to whether I had it in me to bounce back.

My test results from the bike were pretty poor. All the numbers were low, bar the body fat percentage. In effect, I was weak and fat. I'd reached an all-time low. I wondered if it was the beginning of the end. Was this the start of a downward spiral in performance that I couldn't get out of? I was thirty-three years old, maybe that's what happens when you hit your mid-thirties.

Did I want to be one of those athletes who keeps plugging away, gradually working their way down the results sheets? Did I really want to put myself through another four-year Paralympic cycle to feel like this? Was it really worth it? Maybe it was time to call it a day.

One final shot

In the space of a few months, I had lost my Paralympic title, I had lost both my world titles and I was no longer number one in the country. I considered walking away. After all, I had started the course in Life Coaching and was enjoying it. I had always dreamed of running my own business, so why not now? But something was nagging at me. Almost three years ago, I'd won double gold for Scotland at the Glasgow 2014 Commonwealth Games. It was one of the greatest moments of my career. I was still defending champion and in one year the next Commonwealth Games would take place on the Gold Coast, Australia. The thought of sitting at home watching someone take my titles, without even putting up a fight, definitely didn't appeal. I made the decision to give it one more year, one more crack. One year felt a more manageable commitment than the four-year cycle until the next Paralympic Games.

I made that decision. I got back into training and began to shift some of the weight. I would have to if I wanted to defend my titles at the Gold Coast. I started doing endurance training, not one of my strengths. The goal was to get in shape and get fit, and I needed to reduce my body fat percentage. The first week or two of rides were tough. Although I had a new focus, I wasn't totally committed at this point. I'd sit on the static training bike at home and ride for one to two hours. My mind would wander, and I'd think about getting off the bike. What kept me motivated was grabbing the fat around my belly. When I felt my motivation slip, I'd grab my love handles to remind myself just why I was doing this. I'd got myself into this situation: now I needed to solve it. I was essentially punishing myself. Marketing experts say that people are motivated to buy things that either remove an irritation from their lives or give them pleasure. I was using my fat as my motivational tool, staying on the bike was the best way to remove it. I don't necessarily recommend fat-grabbing as the ideal form of motivation, but it worked for me. This was definitely the case of stick rather than the carrot. I saw some slight improvement over the next couple of weeks, but not the instant success I was hoping for. It was going to be a slow process.

That summer the UCI decided to announce another Track World Championships, this time thankfully with more than seven weeks' notice. We were informed that ten days before the Commonwealth Games on the Gold Coast, we would be competing in the World Championships. Unbelievably we were heading back to Rio for them, the place where it all started falling apart. My instant reaction was disappointment, too many bad memories. I didn't want to end my career with another failure in Rio. There were two tracks where I had never won a race, one was Los Angeles, where I competed twice in the World Champs, and Rio. What if I had unlucky tracks where I was never destined to win?

I started to come around to the idea. A small seed in my brain was asking, 'Wouldn't it be incredible to go back there and lay the ghost to rest?' The seed grew into excitement. I had the opportunity to go back and right the wrongs of 2016. Not only would I have the chance to defend my Commonwealth titles, but also regain the World titles. Win not one, but two, rainbow-striped jerseys. I could earn my stripes.

The gear change in my motivation was evident. I had acquired a steely determination. Over the years I had learnt a lot about how to achieve a big goal. It was time to call on those skills. I had found my drive – Stripe One. Now I had to plan how to go about it – Stripe Two. I sat down with my team of experts – Stripe Three –and discussed how to get me back in shape so that I could step up to a new level. As a team, we discussed how we would select the tandem pairings. There would be a trial process towards the end of the year. The trial would be crucial to my success and so I focused everything on it.

The training was still hard, especially the endurance work. Spending hours on the bike with aching legs isn't my idea of fun. Your brain is constantly reminding you that you could simply stop pedalling, climb off the bike and lie on the sofa. Maybe stick on the telly and grab a snack – bliss. I used a lot of self-talk during those sessions. I'd approach it from different angles. Sometimes I'd get frustrated with myself, pointing out that I needed to lose this weight. I would also remind myself of what was at stake. I constantly repeated my mantra. The go-to phrase became 'Earn Your Stripes'. Whenever I wanted to give up, I'd say to myself, 'Come on Neil, earn your stripes.' Sometimes I would say it out loud. My focus would immediately snap back to what needed doing. I knew I had to push myself harder – beyond anything I'd done before. I knew I had my mindset under control – Stripe Four.

I gradually began seeing some improvement. I set myself targets: reduce my fat percentage measurements every four weeks, increase my power output on the bike over three- and twelve-minute tests. The improvements were never enormous, but they were consistent, and kept me motivated to keep pushing on. I became more sensible with my diet, which had suffered during my down period. The weight started dropping and my fitness started picking up. I was back in the gym and lifting heavy weights. I set myself gym targets. I'd aim to do x amount of reps at a weight of y. All these small improvements meant I was getting faster on the bike. Whenever the going got tough – which was often – I'd repeat my mantra, 'Earn your stripes'. Deep down I knew that this was my last chance. One last opportunity to truly leave a legacy. Isn't that what everyone hopes for? I wanted to be known as one of the greatest tandem riders of all time, I wanted to be known as a fighter and I wanted to push the sport to new limits. It was now or never.

By the end of the summer we were getting ready to race. The trial would take place over two events, the Glasgow Sprint Grand Prix at the end of September and the Manchester Paracycling International in late November. I would ride with Matt in Glasgow and with Pete in Manchester. James would ride with Pete in Glasgow and Matt in Manchester. The process involved calculating the time difference between each pairing at each event; whichever pair won by the biggest margin was selected. We arrived in Glasgow the day before the event. I was nervous. I hadn't raced since the World Championships in Los Angeles and hadn't won a race since before the Rio Paralympics. If I was going to win this trial, I needed not just to win but win by as big a margin as I could. I spent the day planning every detail and staying as calm as I could. I visualised the race several times during the day, I knew every single step. Although it was one of the smallest events I would be racing in that year, it carried the most weight.

I arrived at the Sir Chris Hoy velodrome on race day and it felt like home. This was where I won double gold for Scotland at Glasgow 2014. This wasn't one of my unlucky velodromes. I used that thought to remind myself of what I can achieve. I remembered the capacity crowd erupting as we took gold. This crowd might not be as big, but I had the motivation anyway. I used the significance of the situation and all it stood for. I knew what was on the line and, although I was scared, I was ready. I embraced the fear and channelled it. It was time to perform – Stripe Five.

A time of 61.077 was enough to take the win. An issue with James' handlebars on the start line meant the other pair had a poor ride. Their time of 63.102 meant we had won by over two seconds. The gap was so substantial the selection process had effectively been decided. It was inconceivable that we would lose by that margin in Manchester, but anything can happen. I didn't just want to be on the fastest bike, though, my goal was to win both races. I wanted to be the fastest outright.

Back in Manchester, I continued to work hard. Although things had gone well in Glasgow, I was determined to push on. Switching pilots is always tricky. It takes a few training sessions to get in sync with someone, even when you've ridden with them for years. When you ride with someone completely new it can take months. Pete and I soon rediscovered our rhythm. Pete was keen to make up for the disappointing performance in Glasgow. We were both determined to prove a point at the Manchester event. There was a strong field. The Paralympic Champion, Tristan Bangma from the Netherlands, the World Champion James Ball, and me, the Commonwealth Champion and world record holder. We would be going head-to-head (-to-head!). This was a chance for me to test where I stacked up on the world stage.

I knew that both British tandems would be fast. The Dutch bike was going well, too. But would it be gold, silver or bronze? The Dutch bike went before us and clocked an impressive time of 61.553 seconds. I wasn't sure what Pete and I were capable of, but it was somewhere around that mark. I went through my usual pre-race rituals, getting myself fired up for the occasion. This was a great opportunity to shine on the world stage. We rode well, better than expected, clocking a time of 61.02 seconds to take the lead. Just one bike to go. James and Matt were last to race as James was reigning World Champion. Pete and I watched closely as the splits appeared on the scoreboard every half lap. Lap one, we were 0.06 slower. Lap two the gap grew a little. Lap three we were almost identical. Lap four saw us starting to pull back time. It was going to be tight. They crossed the line in a time of 60.87 seconds, just beating us by 0.15 seconds. It was disappointing to get so close, but not quite close enough. I knew that Matt and I would be riding together for the World Championships and Commonwealth Games.

The following day was the sprint. As it's not in the Paralympics, it has a more fun feel to it. It panned out to be probably the greatest sprint day of my life. We qualified second fastest, just a fraction of a second slower than Matt and James. While they got a bye in the quarterfinals, we raced against another British pair, winning two–nil in the best of three encounter. In the semi-finals we were up against the Dutch pair. These two guys seemed to have no weaknesses and were in great form. We won the first match by a whisker. In the second ride we came down the home straight side-by-side. We lunged for the line and I was certain we'd just pipped them, but a photo-finish said otherwise. It went to a decider. It was another close, hard-fought encounter. It went down to the wire, but Pete and I just managed to edge it.

We had taken the tough route to the final; the epic battle with the Dutch had taken its toll. We would meet James and Matt in the final. Their journey had been much more straightforward. I badly wanted this win. The first match saw us soundly beaten. It looked like the writing was on the wall. I prepared myself for a two–nil defeat. Pete and I talked tactics and devised a plan. Pete is an immensely strong rider, but his ultimate strength lies in sprint tactics. He absolutely nailed it and we edged the second ride to take it to a decider. In the final ride we won more comfortably than I expected. We roared as we crossed the finish line. It was one of the most fulfilling sprint victories of my career.

With less than four months until the World Championships, it was time to knuckle down. The trial had gone perfectly to plan – I would ride with Matt. That was just the first part of the plan, the real task was winning back the rainbow stripes, as well as defending my Commonwealth titles. We sat down as a group (Matt, our coaches, support staff and I) and planned things out – everything geared towards gold.

I was putting my five-stripe plan into action. I had my drive; the performance element was all planned out; my support network was in place and on side; I knew how to control my mindset, particularly using my mantra; all that remained was to perform under the highest pressure. I had to finish the job and earn my stripes.

Two golden weeks

The run-up to the Championships went to plan. We were acutely aware that Pete and James were matching us in training. Even though Matt and I had won the selection process, it wasn't going to be straightforward. The ambitious target I'd set myself was on a Note on my phone so that I could refer to it every day. It read: '4 events, 4 golds, break the 60-second barrier in the 1km TT.' I knew it was a big ask, winning all four races in the space of ten days, in two venues on opposite sides of the globe. I hadn't got close to breaking the 60-second barrier at sea level since the Rio Paralympics.

We arrived in Rio a week before racing began. The airport looked very familiar. On the way to our hotel, next to the Olympic Park, we passed the athletes' village, where I had stayed just eighteen months previously. The memories came flooding back. The Olympic park looked like a ghost town; it lacked the vibrant, bustling excitement of the Paralympics.

The following day we went to the velodrome. Most of the interior had been stripped away and it felt like an industrial shed. There were huge black, sooty marks on the ceiling from recent fires. It felt strange to be back.

The first training session went as expected; the long flight to Rio had definitely taken its toll. The following day I was back firing on all cylinders and raring to go. Unfortunately, one of our starts resulted in the chain snapping. The sudden release in tension caused Matt to hit his knee on his handlebars. As it was painful, we decided to call the remainder of that session off. We headed back to the hotel so Matt could ice his leg and recover. Despite the pain, we managed to complete the next day's session. The plan had been for this to be an easy day. It was necessary to tweak our training schedule in the last few days before race day. It might not have been the perfect run in, but it hadn't impacted our plans too much.

I started to develop a strange pain in my hip. I didn't recall doing anything to cause it and wondered if it wasn't just one of those tricks the mind plays in the run-up to an important event. Was it the self-sabotage effect, making me think I'm injured when I'm fine? I went to see our physio. She couldn't pinpoint what had caused it either, but we started treatment. The following day, and with just two days left until race day, I was struggling to walk. I'd put in all that hard work, fought back from the brink and now it looked like I couldn't complete the job. Was the curse of Rio about to strike again? I did everything to recover: sessions with the physio, stretching, icing and plenty of rest. I was giving up all hope of being pain free come race day. It was my last chance and I knew, if I had to, I could ride through the pain. The adrenaline would carry me through. The next day the relief was immense; the pain had disappeared. One day until race day and suddenly things were falling back into place.

We weren't racing until early evening, which meant another long day sitting around in a hotel room. It was very quiet. Matt and I weren't saying much, it was all about keeping things calm. I distracted myself with audiobooks and music. I had my day all planned out and written on my phone to refer to. Eating is always the hard part, I never feel hungry on race day and food becomes a chore, but I had to force myself to eat what was necessary. Time ticked slowly by, I packed my bag, collected my bike and made the short trip to the velodrome.

Here I was again to compete in the one-kilometre time trial, the very same event I'd lost in 2016. While the memories remained, so did the lessons I'd learnt from it. This was another day and I had a target to hit. I glanced at my phone, '4 gold medals.' I needed a win here so that I could prove to the world that I had what it takes. I began my warm-up. It was incredibly hot, I asked for a fan. 'Relax Neil, you've raced in harder conditions than this before and won,' I told myself. I remembered competing in 42° Celsius at altitude in Mexico. I maintained a calm determination as I went through my usual warm-up protocol.

I finished the warm-up feeling strong, ready, anxious. The pressure was on – this meant so much to me. The event was underway and there had been no seriously quick times; but next up were the Dutch. A strong ride with an incredible last lap saw them clock a time of 60.755 seconds. It was faster than either British tandem had gone all season. We were next to go. I made my way towards the start, having psyched myself up for this moment. Then the niggling thoughts started to creep in, 'What if the chain snaps, what if you don't win, what if Rio beats you again?' I ignored the thoughts and got on the bike. The countdown clock started ticking.

-15 seconds: 'Earn your stripes, come on Neil, earn your stripes.'

-10 seconds: 'No going back now, come on, you've got this.'

-5 seconds: 'You can do this.'

-4 seconds: 'Attack the start.'

-3 seconds: 'Give it everything.'

-2 seconds: 'Come on!'

-1 second: Breathe in

The opening lap felt incredibly strong, there was no doubt about our commitment, we were giving this everything. Our opening lap time of 18.5 seconds was similar to the Paralympics. I felt much stronger this time; we continued to accelerate. After two laps I settled into my rhythm, 'strong and smooth', I told myself. The third lap felt good. Just one lap to go. Inevitably we began to fade. We came around the final bend and lunged for the line. A time of 59.686 seconds. We had done it! 'Come on!' I roared with what remaining energy I had. The 60-second barrier had been broken, my first time at sea level. I had achieved one of my goals. The gold medal wasn't in the bag though. Defending champion James still had to ride.

The adrenaline was coursing through my body. In stark contrast to eighteen months earlier, I was on my feet and I felt good. I watched from track centre as Pete and James started their ride, their own quest for glory. Pete was also determined to right the wrongs from the Paralympics, but only one of us would be able to do it. Would it be me or would it be Pete? After one lap we were over three tenths of a second ahead, after two laps it was almost five tenths. The gap continued to grow, and the pair came round in a time of 60.535 seconds – good enough for silver. We had won by almost a second. Where did that come from? Our times had been so close to our teammates in training, yet we'd found something extra from somewhere. All that hard work, pain, heartache, suffering and dedication had all been for this. I was a World Champion again – I had earned my stripes.

My plan, however, was to win four golds and break the 60-second barrier. With one gold and the 60-second barrier smashed; the show was well on its way. But there was plenty more to be done. The following day was sprint day. My legs were feeling rough from the previous day, but spirits were high. Neither Matt nor I had slept well, but we attacked the flying 200m qualifying ride. Matt looked up at the timing board to check our time. 'What's the world record again?'. '9.7,' I replied. '9.7 what?' 'I can't remember.' We were only a fraction slower than the world record, which I set at altitude in 2014. A time of 9.765 was by far the quickest time by a tandem at sea level.

After qualifying fastest, we progressed through the quarter and semi-finals. Instead of racing our team-mates, as expected, we were up against the Dutch pairing. It was going to be challenging, but we were in scintillating form. Two tough rides saw us win the best of three final. Gold medal number two was in the bag – halfway there. I had put the ghost of Rio to bed. These two gold medals would never make up for the disappointment of the Paralympics, but they allowed me to start forgiving myself for what had happened.

There was no time to celebrate; we had a plane to catch. I quickly got my things together, said goodbye to my wife, who was going home to prepare for the road-racing season. The sprint-based tandems were heading to Australia for the Commonwealth Games. We checked in our luggage and tandems (they take an age as the boxes are very large) and made our way through to the gate.

We had a long journey ahead of us – two fourteen-hour flights would get us to Sydney. I was worried my legs would seize up after a tough day sprinting. I've never been good with long-haul flights as the lights are turned off. My eye condition means that I am completely blind on the plane. It's not a huge issue, but it can make trips to the loo rather challenging.

After another 14-hour flight from Dubai, we arrived in Sydney at midnight and were picked up by staff from Scottish Cycling. Unfortunately, our tandems hadn't made it. We had just eight days until race day. Our initial goal on the first day was to adjust to the change in time zone. This meant staying awake, so we spent the day sightseeing in Sydney. The team was relaxed and enjoying the sunshine, but the missing tandems were a concern. Apparently, they were still stuck at the airport in Rio. For some reason they hadn't cleared customs. Matt and I just had to watch our teammates training in the velodrome that had hosted the Olympic and Paralympic Games in Sydney in 2000. In the space of a few days we'd visited two Olympic velodromes on opposite sides of the globe. Sadly, we wouldn't be riding on this one. With just five days to go, we headed to Brisbane. Although most sports were taking place on the Gold Coast itself, the cycling was based at the new Anna Meares velodrome in Brisbane, about an hour away. Despite staying in the tranquil town of Manly, my stress levels were high. Where was our bloody tandem?

Pete and James were riding for the Welsh team. They were in the same boat as us – no bike. There were four days until we raced. We discussed whether we could find a suitable tandem to hire, one that we wouldn't break. It seemed unlikely. Three days before the Games were due to open (and our race day) our tandems finally arrived in Brisbane. The mechanics quickly built ours up and the officials allowed us on the track that evening. Finally, Matt and I were back on the bike. The initial session was a case of blowing away the cobwebs. The following day was our first – and last – full day of training. We were as ready as we could be.

Race day. There had been a lot of talk about how fast this track was. We'd been fast in Rio; could we go faster here? I wasn't sure how much the travel and lack of training had taken out of us, but we were about to find out in the kilo – the one-kilometre time trial. All the bikes taking part had competed at the World Champs: we knew we were favourites. As defending champion, we were the last to go. The Welsh boys went off before us, 60.900 seconds; slower than Rio. I knew this was ours for the taking. We made our way up to the start line in front of a capacity crowd. My parents had made the long journey over and I wanted to make the trip worth their while.

The crowd roared as I walked around the back of the starting gate and climbed on to our tandem. I clipped my feet into the pedals, tightened my straps and took a deep breath. The focus – breaking the world record. The countdown clock ticked down, five, four, three, two, one. We exploded out of the starting gate and I heard a loud crack. Matt and I both looked down. Matt swore and I knew there was a problem. We wobbled slightly, but the bike seemed fine. Matt's foot had become unclipped from the pedal. Fortunately, it was just for a moment. We carried on, knowing that it had cost us dearly. The opening lap was 19.055 seconds – half a second slower than the week before. Crucially, it was slower than the Welsh team.

The adrenaline surge was massive, neither of us wanted to let this ruin our chances. Any thought of breaking the world record had gone out the window, it was all about victory. I had a target to achieve – four golds. We drove the tandem as hard as we could through lap two, hitting top speed. From there it was a case of hanging on, riding as smoothly as possible to the finish. Would it be quick enough? We rolled under the giant scoreboard and I looked up to see where we had finished. Next to my name was '1' – we were Commonwealth Champions and I had defended my title. Our time, 60.065 seconds, almost a second quicker than the Welsh pair. Had everything gone to plan, I'm certain we would have broken the world record. But that's sport. There had been an issue, but we still found a way to win.

In the post-race interviews, I sound like a miserable Scot. I knew we could've done better. Don't get me wrong, I was delighted with the gold medal and defending my title from Glasgow, but I felt the world record had been in our sights. We decided to make it our mission to break the world record in the flying 200m on sprint day. We had a day off between racing and used it to freshen our legs up. The great thing about the Commonwealth Games is that able-bodied and parasports are integrated. On our tandem sprint day, the able-bodied solo riders were also competing in their own sprint event. It meant we could compare qualifying times for the flying 200m. As well as break the world record – 9.711 seconds – we wanted to be the fastest bike at the Games. We would need to go faster than some incredible riders, including home favourite Matthew Glaetzer.

As favourites, we were last to go; we could get incredibly fired up. We would be running on emotion, using the disappointment of missing the record in the kilo. So far, the Welsh duo had been the fastest, in a time of 10.022 seconds, a fraction quicker than the Malaysian pair. We rolled up on to the track and began our wind up. In the flying 200m you do a few laps to build up your speed prior to dropping down at full speed to the start line. The aim is to be at maximum speed for the entire 200m stretch.

Everything felt perfect as we accelerated around the top of the track, ready to drop down. I put heart, body and soul into the final acceleration, powering on the pedals. I could feel the speed as we rounded the first banking. The back straight passed in a flash and we were coming round turns three and four into the home straight and across the finish line. There was an almighty roar as the crowd got to its feet to give us a standing ovation. I heard the words, 'a new world record', followed by another two roars – one from the crowd and one from me. I still didn't know how quick we had been, I guessed just over 9.6 seconds. Matt shouted '9.568… 9.568!' We milked the moment for all it was worth, holding our tandem aloft in front of the deafening crowd. Our average speed had been 75.25kph – seriously quick.

I watched the able-bodied sprint qualifications to see where our time would place us. Rider after rider went without bettering our time. A lot of the guys went 9.6, including Scottish sprint sensation and teammate Jack Carlin. Then came Matt Glaetzer, the only one who could better our time. He flew around the track in his green and gold kit, to the roars of the Australian crowd. A rocket, he had to be quicker than our 9.568 seconds. Yet at 9.583 he was a fraction slower than us. We were the quickest bike on the day and the quickest bike in

Commonwealth Games history. I was elated. I had achieved one of my most long-standing goals. From the start of my sporting career, I have wanted to prove that parasport is on a par with able-bodied. That day in Brisbane we showed the world what we are capable of – what para-athletes are capable of.

The excitement was short-lived as we hadn't finished racing. The qualification ride had taken a lot out of us. The semi-finals were next, and we managed to beat the home favourites, Australia, by two rides to nil to get into the final. It would take place during the evening session, giving us a little time to recover. We were going head-to-head with our GB teammates, Pete and James: Scotland versus Wales. I knew we had the mental edge to win, as well as the legs to do it.

They fought hard in the first ride, but our speed was too much. At that point I knew they were beaten. I could see it in their demeanour, they would settle for silver. The next ride was another convincing win for us – two straight wins gave us gold. We had completed the Commonwealth double and I had successfully defended both of my titles from Glasgow. We rolled up to the top of the track where my parents had been watching and I gave them both a huge hug. It might have been our moment, but it was one to share.

In less than two weeks we had achieved so much. Four gold medals, a sub-60-second kilo plus an unexpected world record. It was more than I'd even hoped for. It was so much more than just two weeks of hard work: I'd battled back from the low of Rio eighteen months earlier. I'd decided to give it one last go and committed all my effort and experience.

My long career in sport has taught me so much. I've learnt how to get the best out of myself, what it takes to not only get to the top, but to stay there. Crucially, I've learnt how to deal with failures, even ones that felt like career-ending blows. Each defeat and each disappointment were lessons I've taken on board. I've had some amazing career highs in my time, but those two weeks rank at the top. It had been a challenge, but it was proof that my approach to success worked and that I could fight back from the brink, pushing myself to performance levels I'd never managed to achieve. I look back on those two weeks with immense pride.

Conclusion

I've developed and used the Earn Your Stripes method throughout my sporting career. Excel in all five stripes and you will see a marked improvement in your performance. I can't promise that you will become the best in the world at what you do, but if you implement the right tools, your chances significantly increase. Take your time to work through the Five Stripes: don't expect to master them straightaway. In the spirit of kaizen, aim for continuous improvement. Make a small gain every day and your performance will grow, too. When doubts inevitably creep in, remember it's simply your lizard brain trying to protect you from change. You are capable – you have what it takes. I'm a man of small stature with self-confidence issues. I suffer from a degenerative eye condition known as Retinitis Pigmentosa. There is nothing special about me, but I took on the world and won.

A few days after gold medal number four, I flew home from the Games early. I was due to start on a course with other entrepreneurs led by Daniel Priestley, author of many business books, including *Key Person of Influence*. It wasn't until speaking with people from the business world that I began to realise the magnitude of my achievements. During the course, I began to plan this book. By looking back objectively at my career, I realised just how much I'd learnt. Being an elite sportsperson isn't just mastering the techniques of your sport, it's about so much more. Through trial and error, I've developed a system for success and I now feel it's my mission to share it with the world.

One of my huge frustrations is seeing people with bags of potential letting it go to waste. I can't bear to watch individuals sabotage their own careers and performance because they don't feel worthy of success or feel they would not know how to deal with it. Too often, the people who reach the top aren't the most skilled or the most talented; my ambition is to change this. I want to see people who can make a difference get to the top of their industry. Wherever you are in life, wherever you want to go, remember that you are capable of achieving far more than you give yourself credit for. Keep pushing on, keep learning and sooner or later everything will click into place. Nothing would make me happier than to see you Earn Your Stripes.

References

All Blacks, www.allblacks.com/teams/all-blacks

Attenborough, David, *Life on Air: Memoirs of a Broadcaster* (BBC Books, 2010)

Fachie, Lora (2019), www.blindinglygoodfood.co.uk

Francis, Robert QC, *Freedom to speak up: An independent review into creating an open and honest reporting culture in the NHS* (2015), http://freedomtospeakup.org.uk/wp-content/uploads/2014/07/F2SU_web.pdf

Gladwell, Malcolm, *Outliers: The Story of Success* (Penguin, 2009)

Harrell, Eben, 'How 1% Performance Improvements Led to Olympic Gold', *Harvard Business Review*, 2015) https://hbr.org/2015/10/how-1-performance-improvements-led-to-olympic-gold

Imai, Masaaki, *Kaizen: The Key to Japan's Competitive Success* (McGraw-Hill, 1986)

Kendall, Graham, 'Would your mobile phone be powerful enough to get you to the moon?' *The Conversation* (2019), https://theconversation.com /would-your-mobile-phone-be-powerful-enough-to -get-you-to-the-moon-115933

Kerr, James, *Legacy* (Constable, 2013)

Lee, Kate E, Williams, Kathryn J H, Sargent, Leisa D, Williams, Nicholas S G and Johnson, Katherine A, '40-second green roof views sustain attention: The role of micro breaks in attention restoration', *Journal of Environmental Psychology* (June 2015), Volume 42, pp182–189, www.sciencedirect.com/science/article /abs/pii/S0272494415000328?via%3Dihub

Lepper, M R, Greene, D, & Nisbett, R E, 'Undermining children's intrinsic interest with extrinsic reward: A test of the "overjustification" hypothesis', *Journal of Personality and Social Psychology*, (1973), 28(1), pp129–137, https://doi.org/10.1037 /h0035519

NHS Guidelines, Exercise, www.nhs.uk/live-well /exercise

Priestley, Daniel, *Entrepreneur Revolution* (Capstone, 2018)

Rohn, Jim, Facebook, 21 August 2014, www.facebook
.com/OfficialJimRohn/posts/it-is-the-set-of-the-sails
-not-the-direction-of-the-wind-that-determines-which
-w/10154462414660635

Rohn, Jim, '7 Tips For Developing Your Personal
Philosophy' (2017), www.jimrohn.com/personal
-philosophy

Syed, Matthew, *Black Box Thinking: The Surprising
Truth About Success* (John Murray, 2015)

The Toyota Way 2001 (2012), www.toyota-global.com
/company/history_of_toyota/75years/data/conditions
/philosophy/toyotaway2001.html

Acknowledgements

I've faced many challenges in my life; writing this book ranks up there among the toughest. At times it has been a lonely endeavour, but there have been people who have helped along the way. This is my opportunity to let them know what a vital role they have played.

First, I'd like to thank Lucy, Joe, Helen and the team at Rethink Press for bringing it all together. In a book where I talk about the importance of using experts to get the most out of your own performance, it's only right that I thank those experts.

Thank you, Helen, for your photography skills, and contribution to and enthusiasm in working towards a final cover.

Thank you to Steph, Tom and Fiona for helping shape my thoughts into a more coherent and entertaining read. They all endured the first draft, so that you didn't have to. They provided fantastic feedback.

I'd also like to thank Ben and Lara for keeping me on track when I found the going tough or was in danger of being distracted by other opportunities. They reminded me why I had undertaken such a mammoth task, providing reason and logic when my emotional side was trying to take control.

Thank you to Dan for initiating this whole process. He convinced me that my ideas were worth sharing and showed me the route to take. It was his input that was the inspiration for this book. Having a successful author support me was a constant reassurance.

To everyone involved in my sporting career – you are vast, you are many. I've enjoyed so many incredible successes over the years; it simply wouldn't have happened without an army of specialists. They are too many to mention, but I am grateful to every single one of them.

Finally, I'd like to thank my friends and family. You regularly asked how I was progressing with the book, even when my answers were not entirely positive. At times, I didn't think it would ever reach publication. Perhaps you felt the same way, if so, you never showed it. Thank you for the continual backing and support.

My biggest thanks go to Lora and her guide dogs Libby (sadly no longer with us) and Tai. At times I've been a nightmare to live with. Constantly stressed and always busy. Despite this, you all found a way to support and spur me on: Lora by encouraging me to work when I tried to avoid it; Libby for insisting I take her on walks – some of my best thinking time; Tai for reminding me how much joy there can be in the simple things in life. Nothing beats a squeaky ball and some space to chase it. Lora, nobody believes in me the way you do, and none of this would have been possible without you. You are a constant inspiration.

Thank you all.

The Author

Neil was born in Aberdeen. He was a sporty child – his passion for sport thrived during his teenage and into his adult years. This combined with his extremely competitive nature proved to be a winning combination.

At the age of four, Neil was diagnosed with a visual impairment known as Retinitis Pigmentosa (RP) – a degenerative eye condition.

In Neil's final year studying a degree in physics at the University of Aberdeen, his eyesight deteriorated to a point where it was beginning to affect his sporting passion. Neil was classified as being visually impaired. He continued to pursue athletics throughout his time at university. He was offered a place on the British

Athletics Development Squad and in 2008 he was selected for the Paralympic Games in Beijing in the 100m and 200m. He finished ninth in both races, but most importantly, he was a Paralympian, and had fallen in love with the Paralympics.

After returning from Beijing, it was decided by British Athletics that Neil didn't have the potential to make it to London 2012 and so funding was terminated. But in just four years' time the Games were to take place in London. Neil was determined to be there.

In 2009, Neil made his way on to the British Cycling squad, and his life changed forever. Since then, he has represented ParalympicsGB, British Cycling and Team Scotland at many major championships, picking up twenty-six medals, nineteen of which are gold. In 2009, he became a double world record holder and in the 2013 New Year's Honours List was awarded an MBE for services to cycling.

Neil married fellow Paralympian and cyclist Lora Turnham in 2016. Together they set up LNF Coaching – a business to help people achieve their full potential, sharing techniques and skills learned through their Paralympic careers to help others reach the top, and to stay there, maintaining elite performance, be it in the sporting or business world.

Find Neil online at earn-your-stripes.co.uk where you can complete the scorecard.

Follow Neil on social media and share your stories with him at #EarnYourStripes.

𝕏 @neilfachie
in https://uk.linkedin.com/in/neilfachie
🌐 earn-your-stripes.co.uk

Career Highlights

	Year	Event	Placement
Athletics			
World Championships – *Assen, Netherlands*	2006	100m 200m	7th 6th
Paralympic Games – *Beijing, China*	2008	100m 200m	9th 9th
Cycling			
World Championships – *Manchester, UK*	2009	1km TT Sprint	Gold / World Record (WR) Gold / WR
World Championships – *Montichiari, Italy*	2011	1km TT Sprint	Gold Gold / WR
World Championships – *Los Angeles, USA*	2012	1km TT Sprint	Silver 4th
Paralympic Games – *London, UK*	2012	1km TT Sprint	Gold / WR Silver

	Year	Event	Placement
World Championships – *Aguascalientes, Mexico*	2014	1km TT Sprint	Gold / WR Gold / WR
Commonwealth Games – *Glasgow, UK*	2014	1km TT Sprint	Gold Gold
World Championships – *Apeldoorn, Netherlands*	2015	1km TT Sprint	Gold Gold
World Championships – *Montichiari, Italy*	2016	1km TT Sprint	Gold Gold
Paralympic Games – *Rio de Janeiro, Brazil*	2016	1km TT	Silver
World Championships – *Los Angeles, USA*	2017	1km TT Sprint	Silver Silver
World Championships – *Rio de Janeiro, Brazil*	2018	1km TT Sprint	Gold Gold
Commonwealth Games – *Gold Coast, Australia*	2018	1km TT Sprint	Gold Gold / WR
World Championships – *Apeldoorn, Netherlands*	2019	1km TT Sprint	Silver Gold
World Championships – *Milton, Canada*	2020	1km TT Sprint	Gold Silver